The

Word

Understanding &
Trusting the Bible in an
Age of Skepticism

by Craig A. Smith, Ph.D.

Shepherd Project Press

The Word: Understanding & Trusting the Bible in an Age of Skepticism
Copyright © 2010 Craig Smith

Library of Congress Cataloging-in-Publication Data
Smith, Craig

  The Word: Understanding & Trusting the Bible in an Age of
  Skepticism / Craig Smith
       p. cm.
  Includes bibliographical references and indexes.
  ISBN-10: 0-9755135-6-7 (pbk.)
  ISBN-13: 978-0-9755135-6-9 (pbk.)

Shepherd Project Press
91 S. Carlton Street
Castle Rock, CO 80104
Email: info@shepherdproject.com

Contents

Why The Bible Matters So Much

The Bible Under Fire

I grew up in a good Christian home where the Bible was always respected. Whatever else I may have known, at an early age I at least knew that the Bible was Important. You could almost hear the capital letters when people in our church talked about the Bible or the Scriptures or the Word or what my grandparents sometimes called the Good Book.

I also knew where the Bible came from: it came from God; that's why we called it God's Word, after all. I honestly don't know that I ever encountered anyone who expressed genuine doubt about that idea until I got to college.

My first exposure to radically different views of what the Bible is and how we got it came in my freshman honors English colloquium at Kent State University.

I remember that I was pretty nervous on that first day of class. See, I had chosen to go to a secular (i.e. non-Christian) university and lots of people had warned me that the professors there would be out to get me since I was a Christian. They told me that the university faculty would do their best to make me lose my faith in what I had been taught growing up. So, as you can imagine, I entered that first class with a fair amount of trepidation.

The professor wasn't there yet, but a teaching assistant was handing out the syllabi for the class, so I shuffled up and got one, then retreated to a seat somewhere near the back. I started skimming through the class expectations and the reading list for the year. I remember that one book in particular caught my attention. It was a simple, one-word title: *John.* Could it be?

It was! We were going to be reading the Gospel of John in my college English class! I cannot tell you how relieved I was. Here I had been getting myself all psyched up to withstand these vicious anti-Christian attacks when in reality we were going to be doing Bible study right there in class! I immediately relaxed.

It didn't take long, however, before I was all kinds of tense again. Yes, we were studying the Gospel of John, but not in any way I had ever heard of before. This was what the professor called "critical" study, which apparently meant that we were supposed to do at least three key things:

1. Begin with the assumption that nothing the book said could possibly be true. Only when there was overwhelming historical evidence for a particular claim should we ever admit the possibility that it might have gotten a few insignificant facts right.

2. Assume that the book was a deliberate attempt to obscure the truth. In other words, you should probably start by assuming that the opposite of whatever the book said was actually true.

3. Assume that anyone who believed the book was at the very least extremely naïve and probably a little bit intellectually challenged.

Now, as we'll see shortly, none of these things have any place in real "critical" studies which have, in fact, provided some very helpful insights into our understanding of the Bible. At the time, however, I didn't know that. This was my first introduction to what often passes for "scholarly" study of the Bible, and it was absolutely devastating.

There were a lot of students in that class who came in Christian and went out...well, less-Christian at the very least. Who could blame them? When you've got an obviously bright and well-respected professor telling you day in and day out that the Bible is filled with contradictions, inaccuracies and primitive mythologies, how are you supposed to respond? It's not like we had ever heard any of this stuff before. And the professor had an explanation for our ignorance: it was because we had grown up in church where we'd been brainwashed to accept whatever the leadership told us without any thought at all.

I'd be lying if I didn't admit that I was deeply troubled by that experience. I remember a lot of days where I left class all knotted up inside, wondering if this guy was right: was the Bible really just a collection of myths told by power-hungry men who wanted to exert their control over the masses? Had I been fed a pack of lies by my church and my parents? I honestly didn't know.

So, I did the only thing I could think to do: I started doing my own research. It became my habit to go from class to the library where I read books about the Bible. Some of those books were sort of anti-Bible and some of them were more pro-Bible, but over the course of that first year in college, I came to a rather startling conclusion: my English professor really had no idea what he was talking about. Of course, the more Christian scholars were all gung-ho about defending the historical accuracy of the Bible, but my research made it clear that they had very good reasons for doing so: there is solid evidence that the historical claims in the Bible are accurate. What's more, it turned out that some of my professor's "critical" conclusions about the Gospel of John and the Bible weren't accepted even by very obviously non-Christian scholars. In other words, what I had been fed in that class was a minority opinion with a very clear negative bias – a bias that didn't really square well with the facts.

I wish I could go back and re-take that class, knowing what I know now. If only I had gone into that class knowing the facts. I could have interrupted some of the professor's tirades with simple questions: but what about *this* fact? How about *this* evidence?

While I might not have changed the professor's mind, I might have decreased the casualties. I'm sure that some of the students who left that class with their faith in tatters would have been encouraged and strengthened by my knowledge.

But, unfortunately, I didn't know then what I know now. I walked into that class completely unprepared. Not only did I not know the answers…I didn't even know that the *questions* were out there.

I don't want that to happen to you, and that's why I've written this book. It's my hope that this book will be a resource to you, not only shaping the way you think about the Bible, but also serving as a place to go back to time and again to find answers to the kinds of questions that you will face about the Word of God.

Chances are, these are questions that you're more familiar with than I was. It's not that my childhood was sheltered; it's just that the kinds of questions I encountered in college simply weren't being asked much outside of certain kinds of academic settings.

That's really not true anymore. "Critical" biblical studies have gone mainstream. Scholars with opinions very much like my English professor's are everywhere now. They're interviewed by *Newsweek* magazine every time Easter and Christmas roll around. The Discovery Channel consults with them whenever some new piece of archaeological evidence is unearthed. Massive bestselling books like *The Da Vinci Code* have popularized these ideas. Walk into any good-sized bookstore and you'll find whole racks of material dedicated to a new industry that has arisen: call it revisionist history or speculative bibliology or, probably more accurately, Bible-bashing.

My point is simply this: any Christian who hasn't completely withdrawn from our culture will encounter tough questions about what the Bible is, where it came from and what we're supposed to think about it. No one who is serious about living out their Christian faith with authenticity and relevancy in the modern world can afford not to have answers to these kinds of questions.

The Bible Is Crucial

Why is the Bible so important? After all, if you didn't have a Bible, you could still have faith, couldn't you? Of course. Lots of people over the years have come to believe and trust in Jesus without ever having access to a copy of the Bible. So why is the Bible so important to Christianity?

The answer is that the heart of Christian faith is Jesus of Nazareth and almost everything we know about Jesus comes from the Bible. We have a few other documents from the 1st century when Jesus lived that talk about Jesus,[1] but not very many. This is to be expected. While Jesus was the most important man who has ever lived, he was born to poor parents in a relatively obscure part of the ancient world. In those days, the only people who had much written about them were great kings and emperors. Of course, over the centuries, more has been written about Jesus than probably anyone else, but when he first arrived on the scene, the nature of his arrival ensured that only a small group of people would recognize his significance. Given this fact, the amount of extra-biblical[2] attention given to Jesus is actually quite striking. The fact remains, however, that most of what we know about Jesus comes from the Bible.

If the Bible is not a reliable account of Jesus, then the Christian faith is on very shaky ground. The heart of Christianity is the historical claim that the Son of God became a human being, lived in first century Palestine, was crucified under the direction of a Roman governor named Pontius Pilate, and rose from the dead three days after his burial. If that didn't actually happen, the Christian faith is totally useless. In fact, the Apostle Paul, writing to the Christian church in the Greek city of Corinth, said this:

---

[1] We'll look at a few of these later in this book.

[2] This just means evidence of Jesus from outside the Bible itself, usually from writers working within the first 100 years or so of Jesus' ministry.

*"...if Christ has not been raised, our preach-
ing is useless and so is your faith."*
(1 Corinthians 15:14)

Christianity is not about the blind-leap-into-the-dark kind
of faith – it's about trusting in something that you have good
reason to believe on the basis of the evidence.

But where does the evidence for who Jesus really was
come from? Mostly, it comes from the Gospels of Matthew,
Mark, Luke and John in the Bible, so you can see why knowing
whether or not we can trust what the Bible says is so important.

In some ways, the reliability of the Gospels is what is most
important, but we can't simply focus on the Gospels and ignore
the rest of the Christian Scriptures. The Bible is not simply a
collection of texts that are largely unrelated to one another.
No, the Bible as a whole is the story of God showing Himself
to humanity. No one part of Scripture can be completely iso-
lated from the other parts. There are threads throughout the
Bible that weave between the different books. The Gospels
that are so important for our understanding of Jesus build upon
things in Old Testament books like Genesis, the Psalms, Isaiah
and lots more. The other writings of the New Testament are
equally dependent on the books of the Old Testament.

So, if the Bible is unreliable at any point, the truth of the
whole of Scripture becomes uncertain. Similarly, if we misunderstand, ignore or undervalue any part of Scripture, we are
likely to misunderstand or miss important issues in other parts.
The question isn't if *this* or *that* part of the Bible can be trusted.
The question is if the Bible as a whole can be trusted.

Make no mistake about it: while Christianity is bigger than
the Bible, Christianity is absolutely dependent on the Bible.
Yes, a Christian might tell someone the story of Jesus and they

might believe without ever picking up a Bible, but where did
that Christian get the facts about Jesus to share in the first
place? Most likely, from the Bible.

It is possible, of course, that one Christian could simply get
the story of Jesus from another Christian, who got it from
another, who got it from another, and so on, all the way back to
the first followers of Jesus who saw it all first-hand. If that
were the case, then Christianity wouldn't be dependent on the
Bible, would it? No, it wouldn't, but there's an important
question we need to ask: if what we know about Jesus were
passed from one person to another for thousands of years, what
is the likelihood that the story would remain unchanged? Anyone who has ever played the Telephone Game[3] can answer that
one: pretty unlikely.

If the story of Jesus were passed person to person over the
centuries, it would be impossible to know whether or not the
story was still trustworthy. The only way to know for sure if
the story had remained accurate over the years would be to
have a written copy of the initial story to compare it against.

---

[3] If you're not familiar with the Telephone Game, it goes like this: a
bunch of people line up and then the first person in the line writes
down a short message and whispers it to the second person, who then
whispers it to the next person in line, and so on. When the whispered
message finally gets to the last person in line, they tell the group what
they heard and this is compared to the original message. Without fail,
what the last person heard and what the first person wrote down are
very different. In many cases, the beginning and ending messages
seem to be almost completely unrelated to each other. "Let's go over
to the coffee house to try out their new mocha shake this afternoon"
has become "Purple monkeys have a midnight roost in the Poconos."

And that's precisely what the Bible is: a written copy of the story or stories from the people who saw them first-hand.[4] The existence of the Bible gives us the ability to make sure that what we believe about Jesus is based on the facts and not on rumors.

Christianity makes some pretty bold claims: it says that the only way to God is through trusting in His son, Jesus:

> *Jesus answered, "I am the way and the truth and the life. No one comes to the Father except through me."*
>
> (John 14:6)

Christianity also says that the confirmation of this claim is the fact that Jesus died and rose from the dead three days later.

Christianity is a very exclusive faith in that it says the only way to be right with God is to trust in these core truths. Christianity doesn't really allow you to hedge your bets by mixing beliefs and practices from a bunch of different religions. It says that these core truths and these core truths alone can save us. In that sense, Christianity asks a lot from its followers: we must either trust in the Christian version of reality completely or abandon it entirely. If the Christian version of reality is true, then there is no reason not to trust it completely. On the other hand, if the Christian version of reality is wrong, there is no reason not to abandon it entirely.

---

[4] This is a little over-simplified, of course. Not all the accounts in the Bible are from eye-witnesses, but most of them are. We'll explore this topic in more detail in a bit.

At the end of the day, our understanding of what the Christian version of reality actually is – and our decision of whether or not to trust it – depends on the Bible. This is why Christianity is more than simply a trust in Jesus; it is also a trust in his Word.

What Is The Bible?

Depending on who you ask, there are a lot of different opinions about the Bible. To some, it is the revelation of God Himself, while to others it is a collection of myths. Some trust absolutely in it, while others trust nothing in it. Some see the Bible as a great work of literature, worthy of respect regardless of what you happen to think about its religious claims. Others see the Bible as nothing more than the superstitious ramblings of ignorant primitives.

Most of the various views of the Bible fit into one of three broad categories:

1. The Word of God
2. The word of God & men
3. The word of men

View # 1: The Bible Is The Word Of God

For those whose view of the Bible fits into the first category, the Bible is understood to be revelation direct from God. It contains accurate information about God because it came from God, and God is both all-knowing and incapable of lying (Hebrews 6:18). While human beings were obviously involved in the writing of the Scripture, their work was guided and superintended[5] by God so that the results would be precisely what He wanted them to be. Therefore, the Bible contains no errors of any kind and can be trusted in all matters to which it speaks.

---

[5] This is a word we'll look at more closely in just a bit.

View # 2: The Bible Is The Word Of God & Men

For those whose view of the Bible fits into the second category, the Bible may be a helpful source for learning some things about God, but it cannot be trusted absolutely because it is often the work of human beings who can – and frequently do – make mistakes. This view doesn't deny that God exists or that He has acted in history. This view is simply skeptical about the Bible being a completely accurate account of the things that God has done. In other words, whereas the first view says "the Bible *is* the Word of God," this view says "the Bible *contains* the words of God (or at least some of them)." In this view, God has done things in history and human beings have recalled them as best as they are able and have written down their recollections in the Bible. Because humans make mistakes, their memory of God's revelations and their understanding of His purposes are prone to error and cannot, therefore, be fully trusted.

View # 3: The Bible Is The Word Of Men

For those whose view of the Bible fits into the third category, the Bible is nothing more than the invention of human beings. In theory, this view may still allow for the existence of a God who acts in human history, but in practice, this view is essentially atheistic. It assumes that God, if He exists, is largely a passive observer of human history. Consequently, stories of miracles or prophecies or things like that must be the invention of human beings. Why would human beings make up such stories? Opinions vary. Some believe that the authors of the Bible were simply ignorant of scientific principles and so they labeled everything they didn't understand a "miracle." Others believe that the authors of the Bible were trying to set themselves up in positions of power and used stories of miracles and of God's wrath to control the masses of people under their control. In any event, this view believes that the Bible not only cannot be trusted – it should not be trusted. In fact, many people whose view of the Bible fits into this category would very much like to see the Bible removed from modern culture almost entirely.

To be fair, most who view the Bible as nothing more than the invention of men tend to feel the same way about *all* religious writings. Their dislike of religion is not focused only on Christianity or its Scripture. For instance, well-known atheist Christopher Hitchens writes that all religion is:

> *"violent, irrational, intolerant, allied to racism and tribalism and bigotry, invested in ignorance and hostile to free inquiry, contemptuous of women and coercive toward children."*[6]

However, since Christianity has historically been the predominant religious faith of the Western world, most of the attacks on religion have been focused there.

While settling the question of what the Bible is requires answering such critiques, we will save a more thorough response for a later chapter. For now it might be helpful to ask a rather simple question: what would we expect to find in the Bible if each of these three broad views of it were correct?

---

[6] Christopher Hitchens, *God Is Not Great: How Religion Poisons Everything* (New York: Twelve Books, 2007), 56.

What If The Bible Were The Word Of Men?

If the Bible were nothing more than the word of men, we would naturally expect to find at least two things:

1. Contradictions
2. Errors

Let's deal with each of these.

1. Contradictions

Since the Bible was written over hundreds of years by a wide variety of individuals, we would expect their accounts of God to vary substantially. In fact, it would be nearly inconceivable that their accounts of who God is and what He is like would not contradict each other at various points.

Of course, this is precisely what many critics of the Bible claim to find in it, but on closer examination, their claims fall apart. For instance, one of the most common claims of contradiction involves the character of God in the Old Testament vs. the New Testament. In the O.T., so the claim goes, God is a violent, angry deity who is always quick to bring His wrath down upon the objects of His displeasure. Atheist Richard Dawkins describes the "O.T. God" this way:

> *"The God of the Old Testament is arguably the most unpleasant character in all fiction: jealous and proud of it; a petty, unjust, unforgiving control-freak; a vindictive, bloodthirsty ethnic cleanser; a misogynistic, homophobic,*

racist, infanticidal, genocidal, filicidal, pesti-
lential, megalomaniacal, sadomasochistic, ca-
priciously malevolent bully. "[7]

Whew! I'm not even sure what all those words mean, but they sound pretty awful, don't they? Who would want to worship a God like that? But what Dawkins completely ignores is the fact that the O.T. contains some of the most powerful expressions of God's love:

In your unfailing love you will lead the people
you have redeemed. In your strength you will
guide them to your holy dwelling.

(Exodus 15:13)

And he passed in front of Moses, proclaiming,
"The LORD, the LORD, the compassionate
and gracious God, slow to anger, abounding in
love and faithfulness, maintaining love to
thousands, and forgiving wickedness, rebellion
and sin."

(Exodus 34:6-7)

Accompanied by trumpets, cymbals and other
instruments, they raised their voices in praise
to the LORD and sang: "He is good; his love
endures forever."

(2 Chronicles 5:13)

---

[7] Richard Dawkins, *The God Delusion* (London: Bantam Books, 2006), 31.

> *They refused to listen and failed to remember
> the miracles you performed among them. They
> became stiff-necked and in their rebellion ap-
> pointed a leader in order to return to their sla-
> very. But you are a forgiving God, gracious
> and compassionate, slow to anger and abound-
> ing in love. Therefore you did not desert
> them...*
>
> (Nehemiah 9:17)

> *Turn, O LORD, and deliver me; save me be-
> cause of your unfailing love.*
>
> (Psalm 6:4)

> *Surely goodness and love will follow me all the
> days of my life, and I will dwell in the house of
> the LORD forever.*
>
> (Psalm 23:6)

This is just a small sampling. Even a quick search for the English word "love" in the O.T. reveals hundreds of verses which speak of God's love. Of course there are plenty of verses which speak of God's wrath poured out on the wicked, but these are a necessary component of genuine love. Can you imagine a father who said that he loved his child but didn't defend that child against cruelty and wickedness? As a father myself, I can tell you that I would strike out decisively against anyone who tried to kill or molest my children. If I was unwilling to respond in this way, how could I say that my love for my children was genuine? When we read of God's wrath brought to bear against the nations who were persecuting His people, we are really only seeing one facet of God's love. We tend to focus on the people who received God's wrath and feel bad for them, rather than looking at the evil they committed against God's people.

In any event, references to "love" outweigh references to "wrath" by almost two-to-one in the O.T.[8] Does it make sense, therefore, to speak of the "Old Testament God" as a deity of anger and wrath? I don't think so.

Furthermore, the idea that the New Testament presents only a peaceful, almost grandfatherly God simply ignores the evidence. There are plenty of references to God's wrath in the N.T.:

> Whoever believes in the Son has eternal life, but whoever rejects the Son will not see life, for God's wrath remains on him.
>
> (John 3:36)

> The wrath of God is being revealed from heaven against all the godlessness and wickedness of men who suppress the truth by their wickedness...
>
> (Romans 1:18)

> Do not take revenge, my friends, but leave room for God's wrath, for it is written: "It is mine to avenge; I will repay," says the Lord.
>
> (Romans 12:19)

---

[8] This search limited to the English words. However, including other terms from the original Hebrew produces similar results.

Let no one deceive you with empty words, for because of such things God's wrath comes on those who are disobedient.

(Ephesians 5:6)

...in their effort to keep us from speaking to the Gentiles so that they may be saved. In this way they always heap up their sins to the limit. The wrath of God has come upon them at last.

(1 Thessalonians 2:16)

Then one of the four living creatures gave to the seven angels seven golden bowls filled with the wrath of God, who lives for ever and ever.

(Revelation 15:7)

The idea that the O.T. contradicts the N.T. because it shows two different kinds of God is simply nonsense. In both parts of the Bible we see a God who loves His children, but also a God who is fiercely protective of them and a God who does not tolerate wickedness. There is no contradiction here.

When the Bible is read carefully and according to reasonable standards of interpretation, the vast majority of suggested "contradictions" simply disappear.

Here's another example of a "contradiction" you might hear about: what was the wording on the plaque they put up over Jesus' head on the cross? Each of the four Gospels has slightly different wordings:

THIS IS JESUS, THE KING OF THE JEWS.

(Matthew 27:37)

THE KING OF THE JEWS.

(Mark 15:26)

THIS IS THE KING OF THE JEWS.

(Luke 23:38)

JESUS OF NAZARETH, THE KING OF THE
JEWS.

(John 19:19)

Even with an excessively critical attitude it is difficult to see how this is a "contradiction." All four Gospels record the charge that Jesus was thought to be the "King of the Jews" and certainly there is no contradiction about who this supposed "King" was; it was Jesus. However, both Mark and Luke left out the words "Jesus" and Matthew, Mark and Luke all left out the word "Nazareth." In reality, the full wording of the plaque was probably: THIS IS JESUS OF NAZARETH, THE KING OF THE JEWS.

Various authors left out bits of the whole message for some reason, quite possibly due to the fact that papyrus was quite expensive and so things that were not considered essential to getting the point across were not given valuable space on the scrolls. But does one author omitting a bit of information that another includes constitute a contradiction? It does not.

We'll look at a few more of these claims of contradiction later in the book, but for now, let me just say this: if the Bible were merely the words of men, we would expect contradictions to appear all throughout it. And yet, this is not what we find. Instead, though written over hundreds of years by different authors from radically different backgrounds, the Bible presents an astoundingly unified picture of God, His nature and His activities. This is not what we would expect to find from a merely human book.

2. Inaccuracies

Human beings make mistakes. So, if the Bible were merely the product of human effort, we would expect to find inaccuracies. In fact, given the period of time that the Bible covers, and the fact that the authors had no access to modern record-keeping or research tools, we would expect to find a great many such inaccuracies. But do we?

The historical accuracy of the Bible has been a source of consistent frustration to its critics over the years. In fact, where the data necessary for verifying the accuracy of the Bible has been available, the biblical claims have been shown to be accurate without exception.

Now, this doesn't mean that every claim in the Bible has been shown to be accurate. In many cases, the Bible makes claims that we simply don't have any data available by which to verify the accuracy of the Bible one way or the other. But where such data is available, the Bible has always been shown to be accurate. In fact, many of the cases which have been advanced as evidence of inaccuracy in the Bible have turned out to confirm the opposite: that the Bible was right all along.

For instance, the Bible speaks consistently of David as the greatest of the Israelite kings, but for many years, David was thought to be a myth. Critics pointed to the lack of evidence for David as a real historical person as proof that the Bible contained a serious inaccuracy. But in recent years, several archaeological discoveries have made it increasingly certain that David was a real historical king. Chief among these discoveries is a 9th-century B.C. Aramaen stele[9] containing a reference to the "house of David."[10] In even more recent news, it appears that an archaeologist names Eliat Mazar has uncovered David's palace outside of Jerusalem by paying attention to some subtle references in the Bible.[11]

This sort of pattern has been repeated over and over again through the centuries: what critical scholars dismissed as historical inaccuracy and even pure myth in the Bible has been shown by new evidence to be completely accurate. Again, this does not mean that every claim of the Bible has been proven because of archaeological evidence. However, when the Bible has been verified, every time such verification is possible (given the available evidence), does it make sense to continue to adopt a highly skeptical attitude towards its claims?

If the Bible were merely the product of human invention, we would expect to find many inaccuracies, but the opposite is true: we have yet to find a single confirmed inaccuracy. Time

---

[9] What, you don't know what a stele is? Weird. I thought that was basic Sunday-school stuff. Ok, a stele is a slab of stone or wood, put up for a funeral or to commemorate some other kind of important occasion.

[10] Avraham Biran and Joseph Naveh, "An Aramaic Stele Fragment from Tel Dan," *Israel Exploration Journal* 43 (1993), 81-98.

[11] Eilat Mazar, "Did I Find King David's Palace?", *Biblical Archaeology Review* 32:1 (2006), 16-27, 70.

and again, charges of biblical inaccuracy have fallen apart in the light of new evidence that confirms the Bible's claims. We'll look at a few more of these challenges as we work through other issues here in this book.

If the Bible was merely the word of men, we would know what to expect, yet those expectations are not met by what we actually find in the Bible. Therefore, the idea that the Bible is only the word of men does not seem to be borne out by the evidence.

What If The Bible Were The Word Of Men and God?

If the Bible were the word of men and God, we would expect that it would have both human elements and divine elements. In other words, we would expect that it would have both a *natural* and a *supernatural* character.

Now, in some sense, this is exactly what we find in the Bible, but not in quite the way we mean it in this category. If by "natural" we only meant that it shows evidence that God used real human beings to write the Bible and that their individual personalities, gifts and talents can be discerned in the stuff they wrote, then we certainly do find evidence of this in the Bible. But that's not how we're using "natural" here. Here, by "natural," we mean what we discussed above: filled with contradictions and inaccuracies. In that sense, as we just saw, the Bible does not appear to be the word of men.

Typically, when people say that the Bible is the word of God and the word of men, they mean that human beings were just writing down what they remembered of God's miracles, prophecies and activities in history, and that their accounts will be flawed because human beings make mistakes.

I remember a church leader once telling me that he believed that the Bible was the "Word of God" but not the "words of God." What this man meant was that he believed God had really been involved in human history and that the Bible described real supernatural events, but that the biblical accounts could not be trusted because they had been written down by human beings who made mistakes. However, since these supposed mistakes (contradictions, inaccuracies) never seem to stand up to the light of evidence, I don't think this view is true. Instead of being partly right and partly wrong, the Bible seems to be right every single time, which is quite difficult to explain if it is really the work of human beings to a significant degree. Therefore, the idea that the Bible is the Word of God and the word (or words) of men doesn't seem like the best option to me.

What If The Bible Were The Word Of God?

If the Bible were the Word of God, there are several things we would expect it to be:

1. Accurate
2. Consistent
3. Supernatural
4. Life-Changing
5. Lasting
6. Incomprehensible (at least a little bit)

1. Accurate

Since an all-powerful, all-knowing being wouldn't make mistakes, we would expect anything God produced to be accurate, down to the last detail. As discussed above, the Bible passes the test of historical accuracy. Sometimes it does it in ways that are quite spectacular. For instance, a recent study has tabulated the popularity of Jewish names in first century Palestine and discovered that the frequency of names outside the Bible almost perfectly matches the frequency of those same names in the Gospels. An example would be the name *Simon* which was the most popular name for Jewish males in Palestine in the 1st century and it is the most frequently-occurring name in the New Testament as well.[12] Since there is no evidence whatsoever that anyone in the ancient world was interested in following such things as the popularity of various names, the only way to account for this is to assume that the New Testament was simply accurately reporting the names of actual people from that time period.

2. Consistent

Even though human authors were used to write Scripture, if God was ultimately responsible for the text of the Bible, we would expect to find that the various authors – in spite of radically different backgrounds and experiences – would produce different works that were remarkably consistent in their revela-

---

[12] Richard Bauckham, *Jesus and the Eyewitnesses* (Grand Rapids: William B. Eerdmans Publishing Company), 70.

tion of who God is. As discussed above, this is precisely what we find in the Bible.

3. Supernatural

If God were responsible for the Bible, we would expect it to contain things that are inexplicable from a purely human perspective. In other words, we would expect it to reveal things that could not be known apart from supernatural revelation. One doesn't have to look very hard to find precisely this.

One of the most obvious indications of the supernatural origin of the Bible is the presence of predictive prophecy. For instance, the book of Daniel, most likely written about 500 years before Jesus was born, predicted his entry into Jerusalem down to the day.[13] The prophet Micah predicted Jesus' birth in the relatively obscure city of Bethlehem at least 400 years before it happened.[14] Jesus predicted the destruction of Jerusalem in detail some 40 years before it happened.[15] The Bible is filled with so many detailed examples of predictive prophecy that critical scholars are often forced to argue that these passages must have been written after the events took place, even though this goes against the evidence. Some skeptics will argue, for instance, that the book of Daniel, which contains detailed prophecies about the Messiah, fulfilled by Jesus, must

---

[13] Robert Anderson, *The Coming Prince* (New York: Cosimo Classics, 2007 reprint), 127-128, 221.

[14] Micah 5:2.

[15] Mat. 24:2.

have been written after Jesus' death. However, we know for a fact that the book of Daniel was already in circulation among the Jews hundreds of years before Jesus was born. Furthermore, the Dead Sea Scrolls have confirmed that the book of Daniel was not altered by people after Jesus' day.[16]

Detailed, predictive prophecy written long before the events they foretold actually happened is precisely the sort of evidence of supernatural origins that we would expect to find if, in fact, the Bible came from God.

4. Life-Changing

If the Bible came from God, we would expect to find that it was somehow more than just a dry recitation of past events. We would expect that it would have the power to change the lives of people who read it. In fact, that is precisely what the Bible itself claims:

> *For the word of God is living and active. Sharper than any double-edged sword, it penetrates even to dividing soul and spirit, joints and marrow; it judges the thoughts and attitudes of the heart.*
> (Hebrews 4:12)[17]

---

[16] Sometimes skeptics will try to argue that, while the book of Daniel was in circulation before Jesus, the passages that so clearly predicted his ministry must have been added later. This is what the Dead Sea Scrolls have disproven.

[17] It should be noted here that the phrase "word of God" as used here by the author of the book of Hebrews is not exactly the same thing as

But is it true? Does the Bible have this transformative power? Countless people through the ages have reported that their experience with the Bible confirms that it does have this power. In fact, there are numerous well-documented cases of people who set out to disprove the Bible and yet found that their interactions with the Bible actually persuaded them to become Christians.[18]

5. Lasting

If the Bible is the word of God, we would expect it to have relevance beyond the period in which it was composed. In other words, wouldn't we expect something that God produced to have an impact that transcends any one historical period?

The fact that the Bible remains the bestselling book in the world argues persuasively that it does, in fact, have precisely this kind of staying power.

And let's face it: the enduring popularity of the Bible is difficult to explain from a purely natural perspective. After all, the subjects it addresses, the culture it records and the language

---

the Bible. Here, the "word of God" refers to anything God has said, whether it is recorded in Scripture or not. However, since the authors of Scripture thought of the Bible as having been given by God, this description of the power of the "word of God" applies to the Bible also.

[18] The founder of Harvard School of Law, Simon Greenleaf is one famous example, as is the contemporary evangelist/apologist Josh McDowell.

it uses are all quite far removed from modern life. Because of this, the Bible is not always easy to understand. And yet, people all over the world continue to turn to the Bible for instruction and encouragement. Why is this? Perhaps it is because in the Bible they encounter a God who transcends our particular moment in history, a God who will never go out of style.

6. Incomprehensible (at least a little)

The thing about God is that He's almost certainly going to be so much more than we can fully comprehend with our limited minds. How can we expect to fully wrap our brains around a being that has always existed when our own existence is such a tiny blip on the radar of time? If the Bible is really from God and really describes God accurately, shouldn't we expect to find some things in there that aren't quite within our ability to grasp?

It's important that you understand that I'm not talking here about contradictions. We should never try to explain-away the charge of contradictions in the Bible by just crying "God is supposed to be incomprehensible!" For example, suppose my daughter were to tell me that she was going to her friend Rachel's house, and I later found out she actually went to Amanda's house. While I could say "pre-adolescent girls are supposed to be confusing!" and write it off as a mystery, that wouldn't be very good parenting. This would appear (at least initially) to be a clear example of a contradiction and would need to be investigated. But this example is a different sort of thing from saying that some aspects of God's nature are incomprehensible.

For instance, though the Bible never actually uses the word "Trinity," it clearly teaches several things about God. First, it teaches that there is only one God.[19] Second, it teaches that there is a plurality of persons within this one God: Father, Son and Spirit.[20] Third, it teaches that each of these "persons" is fully God in every respect.[21] This is a good example of a teaching in the Bible that is incomprehensible without being contradictory. If the Bible said that there was one God and that the Father, Son and Spirit were each gods, then that would be a contradiction. If the Bible said that the Father, Son and Spirit were all God but that the Son and the Spirit had not always existed, this would be a contradiction. As it is, the doctrine of the Trinity is not contradictory – but it is beyond our ability to fully grasp.

Maybe there will come a time that God will be able to explain His existence as a Trinity to us in a way that we'll fully

---

[19] Deuteronomy 6:4: *Hear, O Israel: The LORD our God, the LORD is one.*

[20] Matthew 28:19 is one example*: Therefore go and make disciples of all nations, baptizing them in the name of the Father, the Son and the Holy Spirit.*

[21] This is a bit more complicated, and since this really isn't a book about the Trinity we won't go into great detail here. One piece of evidence for this claim is the fact that different references to the persons of the Trinity in the Bible mix the order of the names around so that sometimes the Father is first, sometimes the Son is first and sometimes the Spirit is first. In Greek, the order of the names in such a list is a way of indicating their importance. The fact that the Bible mixes them around indicates that they are all equally important.

comprehend, but I doubt it. I suspect that understanding the Trinity fully requires a mind that is infinite, and that will never be true of human beings. In that sense, the doctrine of the Trinity may be beyond our ability to comprehend both in this life and in the life to come.

Other examples of things in the Bible which are incomprehensible without being contradictory include the fact that Jesus is fully God and fully man, and the question of God's sovereignty vs. human responsibility. To say that these things are incomprehensible is not to say that they shouldn't be investigated thoroughly or that we shouldn't make sure our thinking on such things fits within the parameters established by Scripture. To say that they are incomprehensible is really only to say that we cannot *fully* comprehend them. But to say that we can't comprehend something *fully* doesn't mean that we can't comprehend it rightly *in part*.

On the contrary, the presence in Scripture of descriptions of God which go beyond our ability to fully comprehend, but which still correspond to the laws of logic that God has given us, is evidence that the contents of the Bible are not merely the product of human invention.

In short, the Bible possesses all the attributes we would expect to be true of a book written by God. This does not, of course, *prove* that the Bible is the Word of God, but it ought to make us think very carefully before dismissing it.

On the whole, it seems we are on more solid ground saying that the Bible is the Word of God than in saying that it is the word of men.

The Inspiration Of Scripture

To say that the Bible is the Word of God does not mean that it somehow fell fully formed out of heaven, or even that every passage was dictated by God while human scribes faithfully copied down each and every word carefully. On the contrary, there is every reason to believe that God gave us the Bible in various ways which often involved the personalities and the hard work of the human authors involved.

If we accept that the Bible is the Word of God, the next natural question to ask is: *how* did God give us His word? In theological terms, we have now turned our attention to the question of the *inspiration* of Scripture – by what means and in what ways did God inspire the Bible?

There are at least three ways in which God gave us His Word:

1. Inscription

You might be surprised to learn that there are a few parts of the Bible that God actually wrote out directly Himself! The Ten Commandments are one such part:

> *When the LORD finished speaking to Moses on Mount Sinai, he gave him the two tablets of the Testimony, the tablets of stone inscribed by the finger of God.*
>
> (Exodus 31:18)

Daniel 5 also records an incident in which God miraculously wrote on the wall of King Belshazzar's palace:

> *Suddenly the fingers of a human hand appeared and wrote on the plaster of the wall, near the lampstand in the royal palace. The king watched the hand as it wrote. His face turned pale and he was so frightened that his knees knocked together and his legs gave way...*
>
> (Daniel 5:5-6)

> *This is the inscription that was written: MENE, MENE, TEKEL, PARSIN.*
>
> (Daniel 5:25)

Apart from these two instances, God does not usually seem to have done the writing of Scripture directly.

2. Dictation

The term "dictation" refers to the process by which someone speaks out loud and a scribe (writer) writes down what the speaker says word-for-word.[22]

---

[22] Although we should probably not get too hung up on the idea of "word-for-word" as this is a relatively modern concept. Throughout most of human history, people who reported the words of speakers were expected to get the "gist" of what was being said, but there was little or no expectation that they would get each and every word down on paper.

Anywhere in the Bible that God is said to have spoken out loud and His words were recorded we have examples of dictation at work:

> *When the LORD saw that he had gone over to look, God called to him from within the bush, "Moses! Moses!" And Moses said, "Here I am." "Do not come any closer," God said. "Take off your sandals, for the place where you are standing is holy ground." Then he said, "I am the God of your father, the God of Abraham, the God of Isaac and the God of Jacob."*
>
> (Exodus 3:4-6)

In many instances, prophets served as mere scribes, writing down the words that God spoke directly to them.

> *The word of the LORD came to me: "Son of man, take a stick of wood and write on it, 'Belonging to Judah and the Israelites associated with him.' Then take another stick of wood, and write on it, 'Ephraim's stick, belonging to Joseph and all the house of Israel associated with him.'"*
>
> (Ezekiel 37:15-16)

The LORD said to me, "Take a large scroll and write on it with an ordinary pen: Maher-Shalal-Hash-Baz. And I will call in Uriah the priest and Zechariah son of Jeberekiah as reliable witnesses for me."

(Isaiah 8:1-2)

To the angel of the church in Ephesus write: These are the words of him who holds the seven stars in his right hand and walks among the seven golden lampstands: I know your deeds, your hard work and your perseverance. I know that you cannot tolerate wicked men, that you have tested those who claim to be apostles but are not, and have found them false. You have persevered and have endured hardships for my name, and have not grown weary. Yet I hold this against you: You have forsaken your first love...

(Revelation 2:1-4)

3. Superintendence

While a fair amount of the Bible was given to us by way of dictation, the vast majority of it seems to have been inspired by a process we call *superintendence*. To say that something is superintended is simply to say that it is overseen by someone who has the final say in what is and is not allowed. Think of a school superintendent. This person is ultimately responsible for ensuring that the teachers under his/her authority teach the required curriculum. In other words, the superintendent is responsible for the teaching of the school even though the superintendent doesn't actually do all of the instruction directly.

We have a similar kind of idea in mind when we talk about God "superintending" the production of Scripture. What we mean is that God's Spirit oversaw the Biblical authors so that He insured that they produced only what God wanted produced, but did so in such a way that the authors' personalities and efforts were part of the process.

One of the most interesting features of the Bible is the fact that the personalities of the individual authors are quite obvious to anyone who spends much time reading them. For instance, Luke has a very unique style of writing that is quite distinct from, say the Apostle John. So if you read the *Gospel of Luke* and the book of *Acts*,[23] and compare them to the *Gospel of John* and the book of *Revelation*,[24] you will see numerous differences of vocabulary and style. In general, Luke is very proper; his grammar is always very carefully constructed and his words chosen with great care. John, on the other hand, isn't nearly so precise with his grammar, and his word choices are vibrant and powerful, but with nowhere near the obvious precision that Luke favors.

Now, does this make one author "more inspired" than another? Of course not! This is just an example of God using two very different people and allowing their personalities to shine through in their work for Him. Of course, God always

---

[23] Both written by Luke.

[24] Both written by the Apostle John, along with the letters of 1st, 2nd and 3rd John.

maintained a kind of executive veto power over what His servants were doing so that He could ensure that what they produced was precisely what He wanted produced. Without this superintendence, the Bible could never say that

> *All Scripture is God-breathed and is useful for teaching, rebuking, correcting and training in righteousness, so that the man of God may be thoroughly equipped for every good work.*
>   (2 Timothy 3:16-17)

But this doesn't mean that He obliterated the authors' personalities in the course of using them!

By the way, this is great news for anyone who is afraid that truly surrendering their life to Christ will mean giving up their individuality. It won't! In fact, it has been my experience that true individuality can only be attained when we allow the God who dreamed us up to bring out the uniqueness that He intends for us. Certainly when we look at the books of the Bible we cannot help but notice that their authors' surrender to God made them more – not less – unique.

Now, to say that God superintended the writing of Scripture is not necessarily to say that all the authors were equally aware of the fact that what they were writing was, in fact, Scripture. It seems likely that some authors, such as prophets who wrote accounts of visions they had received, were quite aware that what they were writing would be Scripture. However, it seems equally likely that some authors wrote material with the intent that it would serve God's purposes and people, but without being aware that they were actually writing Scripture that would be part of the Bible. The unifying factor that ties both kinds of work together was the Holy Spirit who supe-

rintended their work, regardless of how aware (or unaware)
they may have been regarding what they were actually producing.

The Inerrancy & Infallibility Of Scripture

In addition to *inspiration* there are two other closely connected terms that we sometimes use when talking about the
Bible: *inerrancy* and *infallibility*.

When we speak of *inerrancy*, we simply mean that the Bible does not contain any errors. By *infallibility* we mean that
the Bible, rightly interpreted, cannot mislead us.

Both of these concepts depend on the notion of inspiration:

Think of it this way: if a particular piece of writing has
been inspired by God in the ways that were discussed above,
then that piece of writing must be *correct*. After all, God is
perfect[25] and therefore does not make mistakes, and He is truth-

---

[25] Like the Trinity, this idea is a bit beyond the scope of this particular
book, but think of it like this: perfection means *complete*. Any being

ful[26] and so He does not lie. Therefore, anything God has superintended will be correct in every way (i.e., it will be without error or *inerrant*).

Now, if something is inerrant, then it cannot instruct you do something that is wrong. It can only instruct you to do things that are right.[27] In this sense, anything which is inerrant is also infallible.

Of course, this does not mean that anything at all that people think they should do after reading the Bible is right. People often misunderstand what the Bible is saying and end up doing rather stupid or even evil things. For instance, people in the United States once thought that the Bible *instructed* them to own slaves, though, in fact, the Bible only mandates restrictions that had to be followed by slave-owners in ancient

---

who has always existed must, by definition, be complete and lacking in nothing. Therefore, whatever characteristics God possesses, He must possess to the maximum possible degree. Therefore, God does not know some things, but all things; He does not have the power to do some things, but the power to do all things (at least that are consistent with His nature and character). This is why God cannot make mistakes: He knows exactly what needs to be done and He can do it with no possibility of failure.

[26] John 17:17

[27] This might seem a bit circular since many people think that the Bible defines what is right or wrong. Therefore, if the Bible defines what is right, and tells you to do what is right, it is really only telling you to do what it is telling you to do. However, this is not a circular argument because the Bible does not define what is right; it merely reveals what God's nature and will determines to be right. It is God, not the Bible, that defines what is right.

Israel.[28] Or, because the Jewish leaders who wanted Jesus crucified said "Let his blood be on us and our children," some
people have thought that killing Jewish people is justified.
These are horrible misinterpretations of God's Word. They are
horrible because...well, because they're just horrible. And
they are misinterpretations because these ideas are not what
those passages are instructing us to do at all.

It is important, therefore, to distinguish between what
Scripture actually instructs us to do and what we might think it
instructs us to do. If we misunderstand God's Word and therefore do something wrong, that doesn't make the Bible fallible –
it only shows that our understanding of the Bible can be fallible. More importantly, it demonstrates the need for careful and
responsible interpretation of the Bible. We'll get to that shortly.

The Authority Of Scripture

One final concept that we often encounter when talking
about the Bible is that of authority. When we say that the Bible
is authoritative or has authority, we are simply saying that we
are responsible to do what the Bible commands.

The authority of the Bible, like its inerrancy and infallibility, depends on its inspiration:

---

[28] It is also important to note that the institution of slavery in ancient
Israel was profoundly different from the institution of slavery in early
America. In ancient Israel, slaves were guaranteed all basic rights of
human beings whereas in early America they were considered property much like cattle. We'll look at this issue more in a later chapter.

Think of it this way: since God obviously has authority over us, we are responsible to do what God says, right? But if the Bible has been inspired by God, then what the Bible says is really what God says, and so we are responsible to do what the Bible says. It's not really that the Bible itself has authority over us; it's just that God has exercised His authority over us through His words in the Bible.

It is important to remember that the authority of the Bible is really God's authority. If we think of the Bible as having its own independent authority then we run the risk of making the Bible a kind of god when, in fact, it is only a tool by which God exercises his authority. It is possible for a misunderstanding of this issue to lead people to worship God's Word rather than the God who gave us His Word. And, of course, what usually happens isn't even that people worship the Word of God itself – they just worship their particular interpretation of the Bible, which is an entirely different issue altogether.

What The Bible Is Not

Sometimes, figuring out what something is becomes easier when we first get rid of all the stuff that it's not. In the case of the Bible, there are several misunderstandings that ought to be cleared up, and this will, in turn, make it easier to get to the heart of what the Bible actually is.

1. The Bible Is Not Simple History, But Theological History

Most Christians want to defend the historical reliability of the Bible, and for good reason: if the Bible is known to be accurate when it comes to history – which we can often verify – there will be good reason to trust the Bible when it comes to spirituality, which is often much more difficult to verify. In other words, the historical accuracy of the Bible establishes its credibility and trustworthiness. Therefore, Christians throughout history have been quick to defend the claim that the Bible contains accurate history.

And, of course, the Bible *does* contain accurate history. In fact, as I said earlier, I genuinely believe that every single historical claim the Bible makes is accurate and without error. However, to say that the historical claims of the Bible are accurate is not the same thing as saying that the Bible is a simple history.

If I say that $2 + 2 = 4$, then I have made an accurate mathematical statement, but does this make me a mathematician? Of course not. If I say that the common cold is caused by a virus, does this make me an epidemiologist? No, it doesn't. Nor does saying that objects appear to grow more massive as they approach the speed of light make me a physicist. You see the point, I'm sure. Someone can make accurate statements about something without being devoted to the study of that thing.

In the same way, a book can make accurate claims about history without being a history book. In other words, a book can make historical claims, and be accurate every time it does so, but still not be intended to be read as a history book. I believe this is the case with the Bible.

Part of the reason I feel the need to bring this up is the fact that history books have a bad reputation. When most people think about history books they think of books that are pretty dry and boring, books that are full of names and dates and facts and figures and times and places. Now, a really good history book will manage to convey all the necessary data of history in a way that will be engaging to the reader and capable of drawing them into the story of history, but such books are not what many of us encounter in our history classes. Because of the way that many people tend to think about history, saying that the Bible is history will cause many people to avoid it like the plague. We don't want to scare people off from the Bible before they've even read it! And in any event, it wouldn't really be accurate to say that the Bible is history – or at least not simple history.

Let me explain what I mean by that. When I say that the Bible is not simple history, what I mean is that the Bible is not – or not *just* – a collection of names, dates, facts, figures, times and places. Its goal is not to tell us what happened in history, but to show us the God who stands behind history and who has revealed Himself through it.

In some ways, the Bible pulls back the curtain and lets us see what's going on behind the stage. Sure, the Bible tells us that *this* event took place and that *these* people were involved in it, but that's not its primary goal. The Bible is far less concerned with the details of history than with the face of God revealed by history.

Now, of course, to accurately reveal God by pointing to what He has done in history, the historical claims of the Bible have to be accurate. In that sense it is perfectly fair to say that the Bible is historical, or even historically accurate. However, there is a big difference between saying that the Bible is *historically accurate* and saying that the Bible is *history*.

The Bible is not simply history, but theological history. It is historical fact enlisted to serve a greater purpose: the revelation of God who has woven the story of His person and His purpose into the very fabric of human history.

Perhaps an illustration will serve to make this point more clear. If there is any part of the Bible that could be considered simple history – that is, just the facts and figures, names and dates, etc. – then surely it would have to be the genealogies, right? After all, what is a genealogy but a list of names?

Well, actually, the genealogies of the Bible are far more than simply lists of names. For instance, consider the genealogy we find in Matthew 1:

A record of the genealogy of Jesus Christ the son of David, the son of Abraham: ² Abraham was the father of Isaac, Isaac the father of Jacob, Jacob the father of Judah and his brothers, ³ Judah the father of Perez and Zerah, whose mother was Tamar, Perez the father of Hezron, Hezron the father of Ram, ⁴ Ram the father of Amminadab, Amminadab the father of Nahshon, Nahshon the father of Salmon, ⁵ Salmon the father of Boaz, whose mother was Rahab, Boaz the father of Obed, whose mother was Ruth, Obed the father of Jesse, ⁶ and Jesse the father of King David. David was the father of Solomon, whose mother had been Uriah's wife, ⁷ Solomon the father of Rehoboam, Rehoboam the father of Abijah, Abijah the father of Asa, ⁸ Asa the father of Jehoshaphat, Jehoshaphat the father of Jehoram,

Jehoram the father of Uzziah, [9] *Uzziah the father of Jotham, Jotham the father of Ahaz, Ahaz the father of Hezekiah,* [10] *Hezekiah the father of Manasseh, Manasseh the father of Amon, Amon the father of Josiah,* [11] *and Josiah the father of Jeconiah and his brothers at the time of the exile to Babylon.* [12] *After the exile to Babylon: Jeconiah was the father of Shealtiel, Shealtiel the father of Zerubbabel,* [13] *Zerubbabel the father of Abiud, Abiud the father of Eliakim, Eliakim the father of Azor,* [14] *Azor the father of Zadok, Zadok the father of Akim, Akim the father of Eliud,* [15] *Eliud the father of Eleazar, Eleazar the father of Matthan, Matthan the father of Jacob,* [16] *and Jacob the father of Joseph, the husband of Mary, of whom was born Jesus, who is called Christ.*

(Matthew 1:1-16)

Whew! What could possibly be less relevant to our lives than this big list of people who have been dead for a really long time, right? Well, if you look at the list of names carefully, an interesting trend emerges: Matthew has broken the rhythm of the genealogy four different times in order to mention four different women:

1. Tamar (v.3)
2. Rahab (v.5)
3. Ruth (v.5)
4. Uriah's wife (v.6)

Now, this may not seem shocking, but there are two things to keep in mind: first, this genealogy is obviously heavily loaded on the male side of things, so why are any women mentioned at all? Second, Hebrew genealogies typically didn't mention the mothers. In 1st-century Hebrew society, from which Matthew came and to which Matthew was writing, it was typical to omit women entirely from family genealogies like this. So why would Matthew buck tradition in order to mention these four women?

The mystery deepens even further when we look at who these four women are. All of them are described in some detail in the Old Testament if you want to read their stories, but here's the down and dirty: Tamar was a woman who pretended to be a prostitute, slept with her father-in-law, got pregnant and then blackmailed him. Rahab was an actual prostitute. Ruth was a nice enough girl, but she wasn't Jewish, and in the Old Testament period, there were strict laws against marrying outside of the tribes of Israel. And Uriah's wife? Her name was Bathsheba and she had the misfortune of essentially being raped by King David who got her pregnant and then had her husband killed to cover it all up. And people say the Bible is boring!

The interesting thing about all of these women is that none of them are the kind of girls you bring home to meet Momma if you're a good Jewish boy. These are the kind of girls that you distance yourself from whenever possible and avoid at all costs. These are the kind of girls that no-one wants anything to do with.

But wait a minute…whose genealogy is this? It's Jesus' genealogy. It's the description of his family tree. Now why would you go out of your way to mention these embarrassing women as part of your prelude to describing the life of Jesus, the pure, spotless lamb of God?

Because pointing out that God used this very messed up family line to bring His own Son into the world makes a very important point: God has a place and a plan for everyone, even for those that the rest of the world wants nothing to do with. No one is beyond the reach of God's redemption. No one has ever been so bad that He cannot turn their lives into a testimony of His grace and mercy.

And you know what's really interesting? Matthew, the guy who reminded us of these women in Jesus' family tree...he was a tax collector. And you know what tax collectors were? They were people that no-one wanted anything to do with. Well, no-one but Jesus, that is. Jesus didn't avoid people like Matthew. Instead, he loved them and gave them an opportunity to follow him and to be part of his Kingdom. And by doing that, he transformed them.

One of the things that Matthew's Gospel focuses on is the incredibly encouraging truth that Jesus has a purpose and a plan even for those that the rest of the world wants nothing to do with; just like his Father. Matthew sets the stage to show us this side of Jesus' character by reminding us that God has a long history of doing exactly the same thing. And he does this with a genealogy.

If you read the genealogies in the Bible very carefully, you'll find that all of them do this same kind of thing: they show us a truth about God even while they recount a list of what looks like simply facts of history. But the genealogies are not simply history – they are theological history. And if this is true of the genealogies, how much more true will it be of the rest of the Bible?

Don't forget: saying that the Bible is not simple history but theological history doesn't mean that the historical claims of the Bible are false. On the contrary, you can't show how

God has revealed Himself through history if you don't get the history right. But the historical statements in the Bible were never meant to be received as simple statements of fact. If you memorized all the claims of the Bible and believed them, yet failed to see the face of God emerging from the tapestry of history described in the Bible, you would have missed the point. The Bible doesn't exist to get you ready for the history category of a game of Trivial Pursuit – it exists to get you ready for an eternity of knowing and serving God Himself.

2. The Bible Was Not Written To You, Though It Was Written *For* You

At the risk of stating the obvious, we need to remember: the Bible was written a very long time ago. Perhaps more importantly, it was written to particular groups of people in very particular circumstances. If we fail to remember this, we will often find ourselves twisting the Bible into saying things that it really doesn't say at all.

I was reminded of the importance of this realization several years ago when the no-carb diets were so popular. At that time, all kinds of people were trying to cut carbohydrates out of their lives. People would avoid stuffing at Thanksgiving and push aside the garlic bread that came with their spaghetti. I even had a few friends who would order burgers without the buns! It was crazy!

Now, what do you think people caught up in that craze would think if you told them that Jesus is like bread? What would they make of the fact that Jesus called himself the "bread of life"?[29]

See, for a while there in 21st century American culture, bread was something to be avoided. But obviously, Jesus wasn't something to be avoided, so why did he call himself the "bread of life"? Because he wasn't speaking directly to 21st century Americans. He was speaking to 1st century Palestinian Jewish people for whom bread represented one of the most basic necessities of life.

Do you see what I'm getting at? If the Bible had been written to 21st century Americans, it would look very different: the metaphors would be different; the stories would take different forms; it would have been written in English rather than Hebrew, Aramaic and Greek. The list of differences could go on and on.

Now, the fact that the Bible was not written directly to us doesn't mean that the Bible is incomprehensible. It just means that we need to remember as we are reading it that it was written to a particular group of people in a particular time and place. When we remember what bread meant to 1st century Jewish people, Jesus' point about being the "bread of life" is perfectly clear. It's only when we forget that the Bible was not written to us that we become likely to read into it, or out of it, things that it wasn't intended to say at all.

The fact that the Bible wasn't written directly to us means that understanding it correctly will require some work. We can understand most of it without any more effort than it takes to read any other book of substance, but we should always be asking ourselves if we need to ask some background questions to

---

[29] John 6:35.

get to the Bible's intended meaning.[30] Sometimes, knowing something of the history or culture of the people the Bible was originally written to will clarify parts of the Bible that might otherwise be confusing. Fortunately, there are a lot of great resources available to help us understand that background. For a good list, see pg. 198.

So, the Bible wasn't written to us. However – and this is a BIG however – the Bible was written *for* us. What I mean is, when God inspired the writers of the Bible, He already knew your name. He knew who you would be and what kinds of things you would be going through when you read the Bible. He knew what you would need in order to be encouraged and equipped, challenged and strengthened. He knew what kinds of challenges you would be facing when you read the Gospel of Matthew or the book of Genesis. He knew what kinds of questions would be on your mind when you turned to the Psalms or the book of Revelation. In other words, He knew everything that needed to be in the Bible in order for it to serve its purpose in your life – and He made sure all that stuff is in there. So, while the Bible wasn't directly written *to* you, it was written *for* you.

---

[30] By the way, this phrase "intended meaning" is very important. We'll explore it in-depth shortly, but for now, it is worth giving at least a general explanation. When I say that we need to understand the Bible's "intended meaning," I am saying that responsible interpretation of the Bible seeks to understand what the author was trying to get across in a given passage. Only when we understand what the author "meant" to say can we begin to think that our interpretation is correct.

The Bible As Sacred Text

Ultimately, the Bible is a religious book, a book about those things that make up the realm of what we might call religious inquiry. The Bible is primarily concerned with questions like "Who is God?", "What does God want from us?", and "What is the purpose of human existence?" In that sense, the Bible is *sacred* – that is, pertaining to or connected with a religion.

The Bible contains accurate statements about other fields of inquiry, of course. Throughout the pages of the Bible we find statements about things that may rightly be said to belong to the realms of history, psychology, science, philosophy, etc. But the Bible is not primarily concerned with such things. It is primarily concerned with God and with helping us to understand how to live in light of who God is.

The Bible As Sacred Anthology

One obvious feature of the Bible is that it is not a single book, but rather a collection of individual texts gathered together into a single volume. In that sense, the Bible could be described as an *anthology*, a collection of writings by various authors on the same subject.

While many modern anthologies gather together writings of the same literary form, the Bible, on the other hand, brings together several different types or styles of writing:

Types Of Literature & Genres

There is a great deal of debate about how many different types of literature there are, but at the risk of oversimplifying a rather complex subject, it seems to me that there are essentially only three basic types of literary material: *narrative, didactic* and *poetic*. I think it is helpful to think of all kinds of books, regardless of their subject matter or purpose, as being composed of these three basic types.

1. Narrative

Narrative literature revolves around telling a story. For instance, someone could say, "If you raise an alarm repeatedly when there's nothing to be alarmed about, no one will listen to you when you raise an alarm about something that is genuinely alarming." Alternatively, someone could tell the story of the boy who cried wolf. While both approaches make the same point, they are quite different from one another. The second approach is an example of a narrative, a story.

Now, we have to be careful that we don't hear the word "story" and automatically think "fiction." A story can be *fictional* or it can be *factual*. What makes a piece of literature narrative is the fact that the things the author wants to get across are conveyed in story form.

2. Didactic

Rather than getting a point across by telling a story, didactic material tends to state the author's point directly. For example, in Mat. 5:3 we are told that Jesus said, *"Blessed are the poor in spirit, for theirs is the kingdom of heaven."* This is a good example of a didactic statement. It simply says exactly what Jesus means without any telling of a story. Compare this to Mat. 13:44 where Jesus said that *"The kingdom of heaven is like treasure hidden in a field. When a man found it, he hid it again, and then in his joy went and sold all he had and bought that field."* This second teaching on the Kingdom involves a short story rather than a direct statement.

As you've probably already guessed, many books of the Bible involve more than one type of literary material. The Gospels, for instance, often contain portions of didactic material (like sermons), even though the books as a whole are arranged as a narrative. However, it is often the case that some books of the Bible are far more clearly didactic than others. The epistles/letters of Paul in the New Testament are good examples of books in the Bible that are primarily didactic, though even they contain some narrative and/or poetic material.

Lists of commands or direct instructions for living are also didactic material:

> *You shall not murder.*
> *You shall not commit adultery.*
> *You shall not steal.*
> *You shall not give false testimony against your neighbor.*
>
> (Exodus 20:13-16)

3. Poetic

Poetic literature is a bit more difficult to define, in part because many of the features that we often associate with poetry are present in just about every other type of literature to some degree. In general, however,

poetic material involves a dependence on highly stylized ways of saying things. Everyone can spot obvious
examples of poetry even if they don't know exactly
what it is that makes the example "poetic." For instance:

> "Get off that ladder before you fall down and
> break a bone."

vs.

> "Get thee down and cease thy scaling, lest thee
> fall and turn to wailing."

In this case, everyone would agree that the second example is poetic while the first is not. But why? What it
is about the second that makes it so different from the
first? Well, first, it involves a clear rhythm. Second, it
makes use of rhyme. Third, it uses archaic language for
emphasis. All those elements together constitute what
we might call "highly stylized" language.

Of course, not every language depends on rhyme and
rhythm to make poetry. Even in English, many poems
have neither rhyme nor rhythm. For instance, e.e.
cummings'[31] poem, "all in green my love went riding"
begins this way:

---

[31] This is not a mistake. This is how his name is written. He's like
the ♀ of the poetry world.

all in green went my love riding
on a great horse of gold
into the silver dawn.

four lean hounds crouched low and smiling
the merry deer ran before.

fleeter be they than dappled dreams
the swift sweet deer
the red rare deer.

This has no rhyming, yet it is clearly poetry, so what makes it "poetic"? Part of what makes this poetry is its rhythm, though it doesn't have the kind of clear meter observable in the previous example. Another part of what makes this poetry is simply the vividness of the imagery and its dependence on figures of speech like metaphor and symbolism. All of these things taken together constitute "highly stylized" methods of communication, and the dependence on such things is the basis of labeling something poetry or not.

Of course, good writing will often contain examples of such highly stylized ways of saying things mixed in with less stylized techniques, thus making the distinction between poetic and non-poetic literature a bit fuzzy at times.

Now, each of these styles of writing can be applied to any number of different subjects, thus producing different categories, or what we might call *genres*, of writing. For instance, one frequently identified genre of biblical writing is *law* or *le-*

gal code. This refers to books like Leviticus which contain statements like this:

> *If a person sins because he does not speak up when he hears a public charge to testify regarding something he has seen or learned about, he will be held responsible.*
>
> (Leviticus 5:1)

> *You must not do as they do in Egypt, where you used to live, and you must not do as they do in the land of Canaan, where I am bringing you. Do not follow their practices. You must obey my laws and be careful to follow my decrees. I am the LORD your God.*
>
> (Leviticus 18:3-4)

While I agree that this kind of material is obviously different than, say, Jesus' Sermon on the Mount ("blessed are the poor for they shall inherit the Kingdom"), both the Levitical material and Jesus' sermon are examples of didactic material as we defined it above. Similarly, prophets who foresaw the coming "end times" and wrote them down, forming a genre known as *apocalyptic literature*, often communicated their visions in highly stylized (i.e., poetic) ways:

> *Look! The LORD is coming from his dwelling place;*
> *he comes down and treads the high places of the earth.*

The mountains melt beneath him and the val-
leys split apart,
like wax before the fire, like water rushing
down a slope.
(Micah 1:3-4)

At other times, apocalyptic literature employs didactic and even narrative material. This mixing of types of literary material can be observed in virtually every other genre of literature that has been identified, including those genres like: historical books, legal codes, Gospels, epistles, genealogies, annals, proverbs, psalms, creeds, etc. Each of these genres that we find in the Bible is ultimately constructed of the three basic types of writings that we outlined above.

Now, while there may be (and in fact are), different rules that we have to keep in mind when interpreting legal code vs. apocalyptic literature, or Gospel vs. epistle, these are, in many ways, secondary considerations.

The most important interpretive differences are not between the genres of books but between the basic styles of literature which make up those books: *narrative, didactic* and *poetic.* If you know, for instance, that poetic material is highly stylized and makes a lot of use of things like metaphors, then when you find statements like "the mountains melt...like wax" in an end-times prophecy, you will understand that this is probably not a literal description. You will be able to make this very important and helpful determination without even knowing all the unique interpretative considerations that come into play when dealing with apocalyptic literature.

In other words, if you know the basic rules for interpreting poetic material, which we'll explore in more detail shortly, then you'll be well on your way to being able to accurately interpret this sort of material wherever you encounter it, whether in the Psalms or the Proverbs or the Historical Books or wherever. The more nuanced considerations that come with interpreting poetic material in the Psalms vs. poetic material in the Major Prophets can be added in later if we find ourselves confronting an interpretive difficulty that isn't already solved by simply realizing which of the three genres of literature the passage is composed according to. This same pattern is true for the other genres of didactic and narrative material as well.

Different Authors

While the existence of different genres (e.g., Psalms, Gospels, Epistles, etc.) is in part dependent on the subject matter of each book, it is also partly, if not largely, dependent on the personality of the human authors of each book. As we said above, God's inspiration of the books of the Bible did not negate the individual personalities of the human authors of those books. Some authors were more poetic than didactic and some were more narrative than poetic. Therefore, different authors produced different kinds of books.

The Bible is a collection of the inspired books of a number of different authors and, as much as we need to keep in mind the different types of literary material they used, we also need to keep in mind the unique features of each author as we read their books.

The fact is that different people use words differently. If a 14-year-old girl says "Today was cool," she probably means something different than if a 57-year-old meteorologist says exactly the same thing.

Therefore, keeping in mind the fact that the Bible contains books written by a wide variety of different people is important. The Bible contains the works of doctors and fishermen, kings and peasants, the well-educated and the not-so-educated-at-all. It was written by people sitting on thrones and people sitting in prison. It was written by authors sleeping in their own beds at night and by authors living as exiles in foreign lands.

One of the most remarkable things about the Bible is that its theological message is unified in spite of this almost bewildering variety of authors.

Different Eras

Finally, the Bible is an anthology in the sense that it is a collection of works that span several distinctly different historical eras.

While the exact date of the writing of the books of the Bible is the subject of considerable debate among scholars, there is good reason to suppose that the books were all written between the years of 1500 B.C. and 95 A.D.[32]

---

[32] Many conservative scholars believe the Exodus from Egypt occurred in 1447 B.C. and that Moses would have written Genesis and the other books of the Pentateuch (Exodus, Leviticus, Numbers and Deuteronomy) somewhere shortly thereafter; Edwin Thiele, *The Mysterious Numbers of the Hebrew Kings* (Grand Rapids: Zondervan, 1983). The book of Job may well have been written earlier than the Pentateuch. On the other end of the spectrum, the book of Revelation was likely composed sometime near the end of the 1st-century A.D.

While the pace of cultural change in these years was probably slower than what we experience today, it would be a mistake to think of this span of almost two millennia as being uni-
form. During this time period, human civilization made tremendous advances in terms of language, science, agriculture,
art, warfare, etc., and these changes are both reflected in the
Bible and important to keep in mind as we look to interpret it.

Again, as with the recognition of the various authors, it is
astounding that a book composed over such a vast stretch of
history could be so consistent in what it reveals about God and
His will for us.

Putting It All Together

The Bible is a collection of sacred texts, written works that
were inspired by God in such a way that the contents of those
writings are what God wanted to communicate, though the
form of those writings still reflects the personalities of their
human authors.

Though the Bible was written thousands of years ago to
particular people in particular circumstances, it remains God's
Word to us, useful, as Paul put it,

> *...for teaching, rebuking, correcting and train-
> ing in righteousness, so that the man of God
> may be thoroughly equipped for every good
> work.*
>
> (2 Timothy 3:16-17)

The Bible is accurate in every respect, but its primary focus
is on the revelation of who God is and what it means to know
Him and be in right relationship to Him.

How We Got The Bible

In the modern world, skepticism about the Bible runs deep. On the one hand, this skepticism focuses on the writing of the individual books of the Bible, claiming that they are nothing more than the product of human ingenuity and primitive thinking. On the other hand, this skepticism looks at the Bible as a whole, claiming that human beings have deliberately ignored, or even removed, important books that belong in the Bible. In other words, modern skepticism says both that the Bible cannot be trusted because of what it contains and because of what it omits. We have already begun to address the question of whether the Bible can be trusted because of what it contains in the previous chapter. Now we turn our attention to the question of whether or not the Bible is incomplete.

When we begin to ask questions about the books that are included – or omitted – from the Bible, we are really asking questions about something called the *canon* of Scripture. "Canon" is a Latin word, borrowed from the Greek *kanon*, meaning rule or measure. To speak about the canon of Scripture is to speak about those books which were measured according to some standard and found to be up to the task, so to speak.

Imagine, for instance, that I needed a set of logs to build a cabin. Before I could begin assembling the cabin, I would have to collect the lodge-pole pines that would form my walls. But of course I couldn't use any and every tree that I came across. I would need trees of a certain length. I might be able to cut some trees down, if they were too long, but I couldn't magically increase the length of trees that were too short. So, I would begin by measuring the available trees and finding the ones that were long enough. The minimum length would be the standard, or *canon*, against which each potential tree would be measured. Those that fell short would be excluded and those that met the requirements would be accepted.

This is exactly the kind of thing we're talking about when it comes to the Bible. The canon of Scripture is the list of books that were measured against the standard and found acceptable. The big question, of course, is this: what was the standard they used to evaluate the books?

Actually, before we can address that question, there's another question that we need to ask, not about *how* the canon of Scripture was decided, but about *who* decided the canon of Scripture.

Who Decided The Canon of Scripture?

Probably the best answer to this question is: *no-one*. What I mean is this: no one person or even one group of people decided what books would be included in the Bible. Contrary to what many modern critics of the Bible say, the fact is that the books that would eventually make up the Bible were recognized as God's work by multitudes of God's people over a long period of time.

This is a fact that most modern skeptics of the Bible simply fail to understand. Consider, for instance, the following common claim as articulated in the bestseller, *The Da Vinci Code*:

> *"More than* eighty *gospels were considered for the New Testament, and yet only a relative few were chosen for inclusion – Matthew, Mark, Luke and John among them."*

"Who chose which gospels to include?" Sophie asked.

"Aha!" Teabing burst in with enthusiasm. "The fundamental irony of Christianity! The Bible, as we know it today, was collated by the pagan Roman emperor Constantine the Great."

I'm not even sure where to start debunking this ridiculous claim. I suppose we should just start at the beginning:

1. There were not "more than eighty gospels" considered for the N.T. If we define "gospel" as a book which claims to be a historical report of the sayings or deeds of Jesus of Nazareth,[33] there are no more than 15, including the canonical books of Matthew, Mark, Luke and John.[34] Even if we expand the list to include other an-

---

[33] I am using a very loose definition here in order to be as generous as possible in my response to those who are skeptical of the canon of Scripture. A far better definition of "gospel" would be something like: a narrative recounting of both the deeds and teachings of Jesus intended to serve as an apologetic for the beliefs and practices of the early Christian community. If we use this definition, there may well be no more than four gospel accounts (i.e., Matthew, Mark, Luke and John). Several of the other so-called "gospels" were written too late to have anything to do with the early Christian community and a few of the earlier ones, such as the Gospel of Thomas, are really only a list of quotations supposed to have come from Jesus.

[34] In addition to the canonical texts, these additional "gospels" include the *Gospel of Bartholomew, the Gospel of Judas, the Gospel of*

cients texts which speak about Jesus but don't claim to be historical records of his life (they are more like the epistles/letters of the N.T.), the list is only 52.[35]

2. Dan Brown (author of *The Da Vinci Code*) shows an astonishing ignorance of the Bible when he has his character say that "Matthew, Mark, Luke and John" are "among" the gospels chosen for the N.T. These books are not "among" the gospels – they are the *only* four gospels in the N.T.! The other books of the N.T. are not "gospels" by any stretch of the imagination!

3. Constantine the Great was not a pagan![36] His conversion from paganism to Christianity is well-documented.[37] In other words, Constantine was a Christian!

Mary Magdalene, the Gospel of Peter, the Gospel of Philip, the Gospel of the Egyptians, the Gospel of the Savior, the Gospel of Thomas, the Gospel of Thomas the Contender, the Gospel of Truth and *Sophia of Jesus Christ.* In the interest of fairness I have included this last one, the *Sophia of Jesus Christ*, in the list though it may not quite qualify as a "gospel" even in the loose sense of the word being used here.

[35] See Darrell L. Bock, *The Missing Gospels: Unearthing the Truth Behind Alternative Christianities* (Nashville: Thomas Nelson Books, Inc., 2006).

[36] "Paganism" is a broad term used to refer to a whole series of non-Christian religions, most of which revolved around the belief in many gods that affected nature in various ways. Constantine was probably a pagan before his conversion to Christianity, but he certainly wasn't one during the time-frame that Dan Brown is talking about here.

4. Constantine did not put together the Bible as we know it. He only demanded that the Christian leadership of his day assemble to settle some doctrinal matters which were causing political instability. This assembly was called the Council of Nicea, which some people claim was responsible for the formulation of the Bible, but even if this were true (which it is not – see below), this would not mean that Constantine himself was responsible for the Bible as we know it! By the time Constantine arrived on the scene in the latter part of the 4th century, the N.T. was already well-established and the O.T. had been established for at least 600 years!

But if Constantine didn't decide which books belonged in the Bible, who did? Again, the answer is that no one person or even one specific group of people made this decision. Instead, the canon of Scripture developed over a long period of time as God's people recognized those books which demonstrated the evidence of having been inspired by God.

The process by which the Bible came together in the form that we know it can be thought of in four simple stages:

1. Inspiration
2. Recognition
3. Protection
4. Translation

---

[37] R. Gerberding and J. H. Moran Cruz, *Medieval Worlds* (New York: Houghton Mifflin Company, 2004), 55.

We've already talked about inspiration, so now let's turn our attention to the other three steps.

How Was The Canon Of Scripture Decided?

Since we've been talking about a claim made in *The Da Vinci Code*, let's imagine that the authentic works of Leonardo Da Vinci got mixed in with a bunch of paintings by other artists. Would it be difficult to pick out Leonardo's works from the other artists? Well, that depends. If you didn't know much about Leonardo's work, then it might be rather difficult, but if you had spent time examining his paintings, then it would actually be pretty easy to pick out his works from among those of other artists. You would simply look for his signature style in paintings.

In the same way that every artist has a unique stylistic "fingerprint" that shows up in all their art, those books which were inspired by God have particular features that His people can recognize.

Now you might be thinking, "OK, but if God used different human authors to write the books of the Bible, then won't the books have their 'fingerprints' too? So how can we recognize God's style underneath the human authors' styles?"

Good question. And the answer is: the artist fingerprint analogy is a bit oversimplified. In reality, the practice of recognizing God's fingerprints on a book was a bit more complex, but the same basic idea I've described here is true.

There appear to have been several features of a book which allowed God's people to recognize His inspiration of it in the first place and which allow us to have confidence in it today:

1. The character of the human author
2. The character of the book
3. The character of the Church's use of the book

Criterion 1: Character Of The Human Author

Anyone can claim that God spoke to them and gave them inspired words to pass on to the rest of us. However, not everyone who makes this kind of claim can back it up. What would it look like to back up such a claim? Well, for one thing, a proven track record of integrity, honesty and spiritual maturity would be crucial. These were minimum characteristics that God's people required of the authors of Scripture.[38]

But beyond such basics, the authors of Scripture tended to exhibit other, more dramatic signs of God's hand on their life. I'm talking about...miracles. See, it's one thing for a guy to say, "God told me to tell you this," and another thing entirely to say, "God told me to tell you this and to prove that I'm telling the truth, He wants you to take a quick look at the Red Sea...notice how it's parting right down the middle where I'm holding my staff out over it. Neat, huh?" You see the point, I'm sure. When someone can demonstrate God's hand on their lives by performing miracles, their claim to have words from Him has a certain authenticity that can't be fabricated.

---

[38] I am not suggesting, however, that these people were perfect. They all had struggles with sin, just like the rest of us. King David, for instance, who wrote many of the Psalms, had some serious character issues that he and God were working through. But that's the key: they were being worked through. David didn't write Scripture as a young man when he was in the midst of serious struggles with sin.

The vast majority of the books of the Bible were written by individuals who performed miracles, or were at least in the center of miraculous events, and this has been taken by God's people as evidence of God's desire to use them to communicate revelation to His people. For the O.T. books, these people were called Prophets. For the N.T. books, these people were called Apostles.

Now, for the record, not all prophets wrote scripture. The O.T. (and N.T.) office of "prophet" is a complicated affair and unpacking it is beyond the scope of this book.[39] In my opinion, prophets were people who were inspired by God to speak for Him, but not all such inspired words were intended to be written down as Scripture.[40] Scripture, whether written by an O.T. Prophet or a N.T. Apostle, is a subcategory of this larger category of prophetic material:

---

[39] One place you might want to look if you'd like to dig deeper is Wayne Grudem's *The Gift of Prophecy in the New Testament and Today* (Wheaton: Crossway Books, 1998).

[40] There are numerous references in the Bible to individuals who were recognized as prophets, but whose words were not recorded as Scripture. For instance, see Acts 15:32 which speaks of Judas and Silas as prophets, though we do not have any record of anything they actually said.

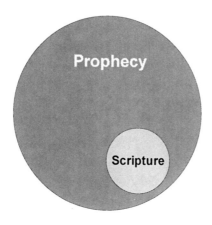

So, not all prophets wrote Scripture. However, most Scripture came from prophets and this fact explains why ancient believers were willing to consider the possibility that their words were actually from God. Think about it: if God does *miracles* through someone, then it doesn't require a blind leap of faith in the dark to think that maybe God is also *speaking* through them.

There's an interesting story in the book of Acts about the Apostle Paul:

> *On the first day of the week we came together to break bread. Paul spoke to the people and, because he intended to leave the next day, kept on talking until midnight. There were many lamps in the upstairs room where we were meeting. Seated in a window was a young man named Eutychus, who was sinking into a deep sleep as Paul talked on and on. When he was sound asleep, he fell to the ground from the third story and was picked up dead. Paul went*

*down, threw himself on the young man and put
his arms around him. "Don't be alarmed," he
said. "He's alive!" Then he went upstairs
again and broke bread and ate. After talking
until daylight, he left.*

(Acts 20:7-11)

So to recap: Paul preached for so long that a guy fell asleep, fell out of an upper-story window and died! Then, Paul raised him from the dead and went back to preaching!

Let me ask you this: do you think people listened to what Paul had to say more carefully before or after he raised someone from the dead?! When a guy who can do miracles says "God wants you to listen to me," you should probably listen. There's a pretty good chance he's telling the truth!

Now, you may have noticed that I've said that *most* of the books of the Bible came from people who did miracles as proof that God was using them in unique ways. I haven't said that *all* of the books of the Bible came from miracle workers. We simply can't say that for two reasons.

First, we don't know that some authors performed miracles. Of course, we don't know that they *didn't* perform miracles. They might have, but what I'm saying is that we don't have any record of miracles associated with them. For instance, I'm not aware of any miracles that King Solomon was supposed to have performed, yet the books of Proverbs, Ecclesiastes and the Song of Solomon are traditionally associated with this man. However, while Solomon didn't actually perform any miracles, there were clear indications that God was with him in a unique way:

*She gave birth to a son, and they named him
Solomon. The LORD loved him; and because
the LORD loved him, he sent word through
Nathan the prophet to name him Jedidiah.*

(2 Samuel 12:24-25)

*At Gibeon the LORD appeared to Solomon
during the night in a dream, and God said,
"Ask for whatever you want me to give you."
Solomon answered, "You have shown great
kindness to your servant, my father David, because he was faithful to you and righteous and
upright in heart. You have continued this
great kindness to him and have given him a
son to sit on his throne this very day. "Now, O
LORD my God, you have made your servant
king in place of my father David. But I am only a little child and do not know how to carry
out my duties. Your servant is here among the
people you have chosen, a great people, too
numerous to count or number. So give your
servant a discerning heart to govern your
people and to distinguish between right and
wrong. For who is able to govern this great
people of yours?" The Lord was pleased that
Solomon had asked for this. So God said to
him, "Since you have asked for this and not for
long life or wealth for yourself, nor have you
asked for the death of your enemies but for
discernment in administering justice, I will do
what you have asked. I will give you a wise
and discerning heart, so that there will never*

have been anyone like you, nor will there ever
be. Moreover, I will give you what you have
not asked for – both riches and honor – so that
in your lifetime you will have no equal among
kings.

(1 Kings 3:5-13)

Even today people still speak of both the wisdom and the wealth of Solomon, so there is clear indication that God was using this man in a unique way even though he never actually performed miracles. We can safely assume that this is true of the other biblical authors who are not known to have performed miracles.

It's also worth pointing out that some books, while written by people who aren't known to have performed miracles, owe their existence to other people who did perform miracles. For example, the Gospel of Mark was written by a man not known for performing any miracles. However, it appears that much of the content of Mark's gospel came from Peter[41] who did perform miracles.

A second reason that we can't simply say that all the books of the Bible were written by miracle-workers is that we don't know who all the books of the Bible were written by. We know who most of the books were written by, but there are a few books whose authors are not clear to us. We do not know with any certainty, for instance, who wrote the book of Hebrews. Many scholars think that it was written by Paul, but

---

[41] Richard Bauckham, *Jesus and the Eyewitnesses: The Gospels as Eyewitness Testimony* (Grand Rapids: William B. Eerdmans Publishing Company, 2006), 155-182.

other scholars disagree and have suggested other possible authors, including Luke who wrote the Gospel of Luke and the
book of Acts. We simply don't know. But the fact that we are
ignorant doesn't mean that the early Christians were ignorant.
On the contrary, the fact that the early church accepted the
book of Hebrews suggests that they were confident that they
knew the author and his character.

Criterion 2: Character Of The Book

To God's people, the character of a book was just as important as the character of the author who wrote it. Apart from
Jesus, there has never been a perfect human being, and God's
people have never blindly accepted anything and everything
that a prophet said as being from God. Sure, Moses might have
been inspired by God to write the book of Genesis, but this
doesn't mean that his shopping list had the same kind of divine
authority! Peter, an Apostle who did miracles, passed on a
Gospel through Mark and wrote his own inspired letters (1 & 2
Peter), wasn't infallible. In fact, Paul said this about Peter:

> *When Peter came to Antioch, I opposed him to*
> *his face, because he was clearly in the wrong.*
> *Before certain men came from James, he used*
> *to eat with the Gentiles. But when they ar-*
> *rived, he began to draw back and separate*
> *himself from the Gentiles because he was*
> *afraid of those who belonged to the circumci-*
> *sion group. The other Jews joined him in his*
> *hypocrisy, so that by their hypocrisy even Bar-*
> *nabas was led astray.*
>
> (Galatians 2:11-13)

Clearly, the early Christians understood that human beings could make mistakes, even those humans that God used to write Scripture! For this reason, no-one blindly accepted everything that a Prophet or Apostle said or wrote as being inspired by God. Instead, they tested their words.

How? First, words were tested for accuracy. Did they match up with other known facts? For instance, when the gospels of Matthew, Mark, Luke and John were written, there were lots of people still alive who had witnessed the events that are described in these books. When such people read the Gospels, they looked to see if the authors had gotten their facts straight. Obviously, the God who knows all things wouldn't get His facts wrong, so no inspired author would make inaccurate claims.

Second, words were tested for internal consistency. Did they match up with the rest of God's recognized words? If a N.T. author had written something about God which clearly contradicted a statement from the O.T., the N.T. writing would have been cast aside immediately because we know that God's nature does not change.[42]

Criterion 3: Character Of The Church's Use

I do not want to give you the impression that recognizing those works which were inspired by God was always easy or immediate. The truth is that God's people were very careful

---

[42] Malachi 3:6 – "*I the LORD do not change;*" Hebrews 13:8 – "*Jesus Christ is the same yesterday and today and forever.*"

about accepting something as being from God unless they were very certain about it.

For this reason, some books of the Bible were only accepted gradually over a fairly long period of time. This was certainly not the case for all the books. Many were accepted unanimously by God's people immediately because of the degree to which they fit the first two criteria above. But some books took longer. For instance, I mentioned above that the author of the book of Hebrews isn't known for certain. Because of this, some parts of the early Church, particularly the Western branch, were reluctant to give it full recognition as having been inspired by God.[43] However, over time, Hebrews was accepted by all branches of the Christian community as they carefully considered the evidence.

Conversely, there were some books that were accepted as inspired by small groups of God's people, but which are not in the Bible.[44] Why? Because the majority of God's people over time judged these books to fall short of the first two criteria listed above. Rather than meaning that the Bible was decided by committee, this simply means that the Bible as we have it is the product of the combined wisdom of multitudes of God's people over the long haul. While Church tradition should never be the only basis for belief, there is nothing wrong with being guided by the established wisdom of God's people.

---

[43] For details, read Andrew F. Walls, "The Canon of the New Testament" in *The Expositor's Bible Commentary* (Grand Rapids: Zondervan Publishing Company, 1984), 1:638.

[44] A good example of this type of book is the *Shepherd of Hermes*.

So What About Church Councils?

There is a persistent myth among modern skeptics of the Bible that the canon of Scripture was decided by Church councils rather than by the organic process of recognition that I've described above. While the Council of Nicea, which met in 325 A.D., is the assembly most often accused of having "made up" the Bible, there are other important gatherings of Church officials that are sometimes suggested as well.

Obviously, since I'm calling this idea a "myth," I don't think that it's true. But is there any kernel of truth to this myth at all? Perhaps, but not in the way that the skeptics charge.

To understand what I mean, you have to understand the context of the early Church. After Jesus rose from the dead, his Apostles began preaching the good news that his death and resurrection meant that we could enter into relationship with God and become participants in His Kingdom, both now and for all eternity. As more and more people trusted in Jesus and became "Christians" (literally "little Christs"), the Church (which just means the community of Jesus' followers), began to spread around the world.

As this movement gathered more and more followers, and more and more influence on the culture, it was natural that some people would try to take advantage of the Church for their own personal gain. These people began to teach their own brand of Christianity in order to gain followers, money and power. Furthermore, these people often wrote religious documents designed to give their teachings validity. Now, think about it: what's the best way to give your ideas validity? Have someone famous teach your ideas! And who was the most famous person in those days? Jesus! Consequently, many of these off-shoot religious groups wrote books where they had Jesus teaching their ideas. Realizing that no-one would believe these books unless they appeared to come from credible sources, the names of Apostles or other famous people from Jesus' day were attached to these books. Thus was born books like the Gospel of Thomas or the Gospel of Philip. These books are called pseudepigrapha, meaning "false writings." They are called false not necessarily because of their contents, but because it is generally accepted that the people whose names are on the books couldn't have written them. In most cases, these are books that were written long after their supposed authors were dead!

However, our ability to determine that these are "false-writings" is considerably more advanced than it was for the average person in the 3rd or 4th centuries. Back then, someone could produce a book and say, "Look what I found! The Gospel of Peter. And guess what! Apparently Jesus taught exactly what I've been teaching!"

Generally, the Christian community ignored these false writings and the doctrines or theological beliefs they were created to support. However, when one of these cults gained enough followers that they began to confuse people, Church councils would make official statements denouncing such teachings and the books used to support them.

In that sense, Church councils did occasionally exclude books from the N.T. canon, but not in the way that popular fiction today suggests, as though they got together and constructed the Bible by picking and choosing from a big list of candidates. Rather than deciding which books to include or exclude from scratch, the Church councils really only said, "Pay no attention to those new books you're hearing about. Instead, devote yourselves to those books that God's people have already recognized." In essence, Church councils were merely defending the canon of Scripture, which already existed, against late-coming pretenders.

In other words, Church councils didn't *construct* the canon of Scripture, they only *confirmed* it.

Recognition Of The Old Testament

As I have already said, the canon of the Bible, both Old and New Testaments, came into existence gradually as God's people recognized God's words. It is not possible, therefore, to give an exact date on which the Old Testament came into existence. The best we can do is make note of various dates at which we have some evidence that the O.T. as we know it was already in existence.

Evidence From Jesus & The New Testament

Certainly by the early part of the 1st century A.D. there was a recognized canon of O.T. Scripture (though, of course, they didn't call it the "old" testament!). Jesus frequently quoted from these Scriptures and referred to this collection of sacred writings as the "Law and the Prophets":

> *So in everything, do to others what you would have them do to you, for this sums up the Law and the Prophets.*
>
> (Matthew 7:12)

This is a traditional Jewish way of speaking about the whole Old Testament. "Law" refers to the first five books of the Bible (a.k.a the Pentateuch or Torah) written by Moses.

"Prophets" referred either to the rest of the O.T. texts as a whole or to the last books of the O.T., thus forming a figure of speech called a *merismus*, which indicates a whole spectrum of things by mentioning the extreme ends of the spectrum, as when we say, "I'd move heaven and earth for you."

Jesus' followers continued his practice and frequently quoted from this collection of Scriptures. In fact, the New Testament, written by Jesus' followers, quotes from every book of the Old Testament except for Ezra, Nehemiah, Esther, Ecclesiastes and the Song of Solomon. This does not mean that these books were not part of the O.T. that Jesus used, however. Evidence from the Jewish historian Josephus indicates that these five books were part of the O.T. in Jesus' day.[45]

This means that by at least 28 A.D., when Jesus most likely began his earthly ministry, the O.T. canon as we know it was already in existence. As a follower of Jesus myself, the fact that Jesus accepted this collection of books as inspired by God is good enough for me, and you may feel the same way. However, it gets better.

While there can be no real question that the O.T. canon was already well established by the early part of the 1st century A.D., in reality it had already been in existence for a long time before this date.

---

[45] Roger Beckwith, *The Old Testament Canon of the New Testament Church* (Grand Rapids: William B. Eerdmans Publishing Company, 1985), 78-79.

Evidence From The Septuagint

In general, when New Testament writers quoted the Old Testament, they seem to have preferred a Greek translation of the O.T. known as the *Septuagint* or *LXX*.[46] From the writings of various ancient historians, we know that the Septuagint dates back to the mid 3rd century B.C. (i.e., approximately 250 B.C.), and was completed by at least 160 B.C.[47]

The Council Of Jamnia

Occasionally, the better-informed skeptics (i.e., those that have read a bit more than the biblical attacks common in contemporary fictional literature) will say that the Jewish Council of Jamnia (or "Javneh") was responsible for determining the O.T. canon. This council is thought by some to have met in the late 1st century A.D. (i.e., 80-90 A.D. or so).

There are several problems with this claim. First, it is not at all certain that there ever was an event which could be described as the "Council of Jamnia." The claim that this assembly of Jewish scholars actually happened was proposed by Hei-

---

[46] *Septuagint* means seventy and comes from a tradition that claims that this translation from Hebrew to Greek was made by 72 scholars working together. LXX is simply the Roman numeral way of writing seventy.

[47] Beckwith, *Old Testament Canon*, 20; for an example of relevant statements by ancient historians, see Josephus, *Antiquities of the Jews* 12.2.11-15.

nrich Graetz in 1871,[48] though there was no direct evidence of such a council.[49] Graetz's theory that this "council" finalized the O.T. canon was a common view for decades, but there is now widespread agreement that his theory is unfounded.[50] Second, there is a great deal of evidence, some of which has been summarized above, that the O.T. as we know it was already widely known well before the end of the 1st century A.D. when this council was supposed to have met.[51]

All together, this evidence indicates that the O.T. as we know it was already in existence some 200-300 years before Jesus walked the earth.

Recognition Of The New Testament

The first book which is part of the New Testament canon was probably the book of *James*, written sometime before 50

---

[48] Heinrich H. Graetz, *Kohelet oder der Salomonische Prediger* (Leipzig: Winter, 1871), 147-73.

[49] Graetz's claim was based on various things that he found in the Mishnaic and Talmudic materials [collections of ancient Jewish religious writings] from which he concluded that some important council must have taken place, though there was no direct mention of it.

[50] D.E. Aune, "On the Origins of the 'Council of Javneh' Myth", *Journal of Biblical Literature*, 110:3 (1991), 491-493.

[51] Beckwith, *Old Testament Canon*, 76.

A.D.[52] The last book, *Revelation*, was probably written some-time before 96 A.D.[53] But when did the 27 books of the New Testament become recognized as a set of inspired works?

There is good evidence that all 27 of the N.T. books were being circulated among Christian communities by 100 A.D.[54] Of these, the most important were almost certainly the four Gospels of Matthew, Mark, Luke and John. At least by 180 A.D. Irenaeus, an important early church leader, would say this about them:

> *The Gospels could not possibly be either more or less in number than they are. Since there are four zones of the world in which we live, and four principal winds, while the Church is spread over all the earth, and the pillar and foundation of the Church is the gospel, and the Spirit of life, it fittingly has four pillars, every-where breathing out incorruption and revivify-ing men. From this it is clear that the Word,*

---

[52] The book of James does not address any of the issues the early church was struggling with as large numbers of Gentiles became be-lievers. This is difficult to explain if it had been written after the Je-rusalem Council of 50 A.D. where these issues were at the forefront. It seems likely to me, then, that the Book of James was written some-time in the mid to late 40's A.D.

[53] Alan Johnson, "Revelation" in *EBC* 12 (Grand Rapids: Zondervan Publishing House, 1981), 406.

[54] David Trobisch, *The First Edition of the New Testament* (New York: Oxford University Press, 2000), 44.

the artificer of all things, being manifested to men gave us the gospel, fourfold in form but held together by one Spirit. As David said, when asking for his coming, "O sitter upon the cherubim, show yourself." For the cherubim have four faces, and their faces are images of the activity of the Son of God. For the first living creature, it says, was like a lion, signifying his active and princely and royal character; the second was like an ox, showing his sacrificial and priestly order; the third had the face of a man, indicating very clearly his coming in human guise; and the fourth was like a flying eagle, making plain the giving of the Spirit who broods over the Church. Now the Gospels, in which Christ is enthroned, are like these.[55]

So here we have strong evidence that the early church recognized only four gospels, and this was long before the Council of Nicea met in 325 A.D.! Irenaeus does, however, mention two other "gospels" – the Gospel of Truth and the Gospel of Judas – which he clearly identifies as the fictional work of cult leaders.[56]

Irenaeus quotes from every book of the New Testament except for 2 Peter, 3 John and Jude, giving evidence that by

---

[55] Irenaeus, *Adversus Haereses*, 3.11.8

[56] Ibid, 3.11.9 & 1.31.1.

180 A.D. the books of the New Testament were already widely agreed-upon.[57]

In spite of contemporary skeptics who argue that church councils, like that of Nicea, determined the canon of the N.T., the reality is that these assemblies did no such thing. They did discuss heresies that were creeping into the church and, in the process, denounced the pseudepigrapha which had been written to support these false teachings, but they did not make definitive pronouncements about what was and was not part of the "official" canon.

If fact, though the Council of Nicea, which many skeptics claim "made up" the Bible, met in 325 A.D., the first full list of the books of the New Testament as we know it didn't appear until 367 A.D. Even then the list didn't appear as an official statement by church leaders, but rather as a simple list of Scripture which the Bishop Athanasius encouraged his congregation to read in an Easter letter:

> *Again it is not tedious to speak of the books of the New Testament. These are, the four Gospels, according to Matthew, Mark, Luke, and John. Afterwards, the Acts of the Apostles and Epistles (called Catholic), seven, viz. of James, one; of Peter, two; of John, three; after these, one of Jude. In addition there are fourteen*

---

[57] Grant, Robert M. *The Formation of the New Testament.* (New York: Harper & Row, 1965). Irenaeus also quotes from 1 Clement and the Shepherd of Hermas texts which suggest that he saw them as authoritative, though whether he regarded them as Scripture is less clear.

*Epistles of Paul, written in this order. The
first, to the Romans; then two to the Corinthians; after these, to the Galatians; next, to
the Ephesians; then to the Philippians; then to
the Colossians; after these, two to the Thessalonians, and then to the Hebrews; and again,
two to Timothy; one to Titus; and lastly, that to
Philemon. And besides, the Revelation of
John.*[58]

Keep in mind that though this list is from a letter written in
367 A.D., Athanasius is clearly referring to a collection of
Scripture with which people were already familiar. So, while
we can say with some certainty that the N.T. canon was fully
recognized by 367 A.D., it is also clear that the canon of the
N.T. as we know it was recognized even earlier than this.

So What About Those "Other Books"?

In the course of our discussion in this chapter we've looked
at a few of the other ancient texts that some people think got
booted from the Bible. It should be clear by now, that's not
what happened at all, but a little closer look at these disputed
works is probably worth taking.

There are essentially two categories of these disputed
books: the Apocrypha and the Pseudepigrapha. These terms
can be confusing because they are sometimes used in different

---

[58] Philip Schaff and Henry Wace, *Nicene and Post-Nicene Fathers,* IV (2nd series), (Grand Rapids, MI: Eerdmans, 1978), 552.

ways. Some people use the term Apocrypha to refer to all the books that were not included in the Bible and some use it to refer only to those books that were not included in the Old Testament. Similarly, the term Pseudepigrapha is sometimes used to refer to all the books that were not included in the Bible or only to those books not included in the New Testament. In addition to being confusing, this is also a bit misleading since it suggests that all of these various writings were seriously considered for inclusion in the Bible when that was not the case at all.

For the sake of clarity, I'm going to use three terms and define them as follows:

Apocrypha: this is an umbrella term which refers to all those books which have at least a superficial similarity to the books of the Bible, but were not included in the Bible and are therefore non-canonical. The majority of these works were never even considered for inclusion in the canon of Scripture, though a few were debated for a short time. The *Apocrypha* includes both the *Pre-Christian Apocrypha* and the *Post-Christian Apocrypha*.

Pre-Christian Apocrypha: this term refers to those non-canonical books that were written before Jesus was born. They do not belong in the Bible.

Post-Christian Apocrypha: this term refers to those non-canonical books that were written during the New Testament period. They do not belong in the Bible.

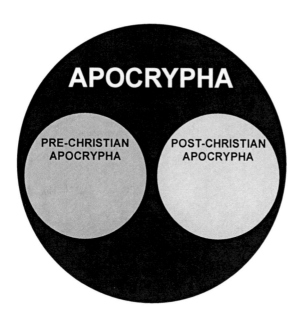

You may have noticed that this list of terms does not include one we looked at previously: *pseudepigrapha*. Properly speaking, *pseudepigrapha* is a term that refers to any text which claims to be from an author who did not in fact write it. In that sense, *pseudepigrapha* refers to any book from either the pre- or post-Christian era that falsely claims to have come from an important religious figure:

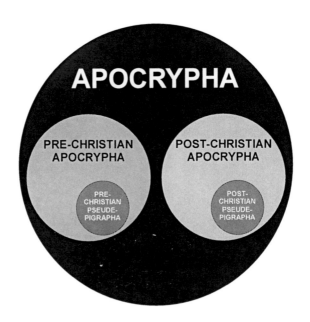

In addition to the pseudepigraphal gospels (pg. 84) I mentioned above, there are also books from the pre-Christian era that claim to be from such figures as Abraham or Moses, and pseudepigraphal letters that claim to be from Paul but were probably written long after Paul was dead.

The Pre-Christian Apocrypha

This is a group of non-canonical writings which appeared sometime during the Intertestamental period, the 400 or so years between the writing of the last book of the O.T. (Malachi) and the beginning of Jesus' ministry.

There are a number of different works which may be included in this list, but the most common are probably:[59]

- 1st Esdras
- 2nd Esdras
- Tobit
- Judith
- Wisdom of Solomon
- Ecclesiasticus (Sirach)
- Baruch
- Letter of Jeremiah
- Susanna
- 1st Maccabees
- 2nd Maccabees
- Additions to Esther
- Additions to Daniel
- Prayer of Manasseh
- Enoch

Though these books do appear in most ancient versions of the Septuagint (Greek translation of the O.T.), there is no indication that the Jewish people ever accepted them as Scripture or used them in worship services. The same is true of the early Christians. In spite of the fact that the early Christian community seems to have preferred to read Scripture from the Greek Septuagint, there is no evidence that they considered these tagalong books to be inspired Scripture. There are a small number of quotations from *Pre-Christian Apocrypha* by early Chris-

---

[59] Not a complete list.

tians, but these serve as illustrations or statements of proverbial wisdom rather than as appeals to authoritative words of God in the way that the books of the O.T. are referenced.

Beyond this, there are other good reasons for excluding the *Pre-Christian Apocrypha* from Scripture:

1. None of these books make any claims to having been inspired by God (whereas many – but not all – of the books of the Bible make this claim explicitly).

2. They contain clear historical errors (such as in the books of the Maccabees when Antiochus Epiphanes is said to have died in three different ways).

3. They contain statements which contradict clear statements from the accepted books of Scripture.

In spite of these facts, some books of the *Pre-Christian Apocrypha* are present in the Old Testament as found in Catholic versions of the Bible. Why? Well, it's complicated, but essentially it boils down to this: though the Catholic Church did not historically recognize the books of the Apocrypha as being inspired Scripture, they continued to circulate in Christian communities, possibly because they were often found bundled up in codices (bound collections of manuscripts) of the Septuagint which the early Christians preferred. As time went on, the Catholic Church developed several doctrines which cannot be supported from the Bible but which could theoretically be supported by parts of some Apocryphal books. These doctrines include purgatory, prayers for the dead and works for salvation, among a few others. In the 16th century, when the Protestant Reformation raised questions about such doctrines, since they cannot be supported from Scripture, the Roman Catholic Church "canonized" some of the *Pre-Christian Apocrypha* books which justified the doctrines. This "official" acceptance of some of the *Pre-Christian Apocrypha* books by the Roman Catholic Church took place at the Council of Trent in 1546.

The Post-Christian Apocrypha

The *Post-Christian Apocrypha* includes a number of different texts, the most well-known of which are probably the "other gospels" like the Gospel of Thomas or the Gospel of Judas,[60] that are so popular with fiction writers and works such as:[61]

- The Shepherd of Hermas
- Didache
- Pistis Sophia
- Second Treatise of the Great Seth
- Dialogue of the Savior
- Valentinian Exposition
- Treatise on the Resurrection

These documents were rejected by the Christian community as they appeared for reasons very similar to those by which the Jews denounced the *Pre-Christian Apocrypha*: they were in-

---

[60] See page 84.

[61] Not a complete list.

consistent with the rest of God's Word and they often contain obvious historical errors.

Many of these texts, particularly the Pseudepigraphal books, were not written until after the canon of the N.T. was already well-accepted.[62] This alone is good reason to reject them.

The Value Of The Apocrypha

While none of the Apocryphal books belong in the Bible, since they are not inspired Scripture, this does not mean that they are all evil or without any value whatsoever. Some of these books are clearly propaganda for cult doctrines, but even these have some use in helping us understand the religious climate in which the early church was established. Sometimes they even help us get a handle on what the early church believed. If, for instance, a Post-Christian Apocryphal book explicitly denies the deity of Christ, then this is evidence that the belief that Jesus was God was well-known during whatever time the book was written. This can be helpful in answering skeptics who claim that the early Christians didn't believe Jesus was God.

Some of the books of the Apocrypha are helpful in the same way that listening to a sermon is helpful. The words of the preacher may not be inspired in the same way that the Bible itself is inspired, but there is value in listening to what intelligent, faithful servants of God have to say. Similarly, there are some pieces of Apocryphal literature that give us insight into the meaning of Scripture, though we must always be careful to test these insights against what Scripture itself says.

---

[62] Bock, *Missing Gospels*, 218-219.

Translations

As you probably know, the books of the Bible were not written in English, or in any other modern language. Instead, the Old Testament was written in Hebrew and Aramaic (just a small portion of the book of Daniel) and the New Testament was written in Greek.

In order for most Christians today to read the Bible, they have to rely on a translation. It's important to understand what our modern translations are based on, because skeptics of the Bible often make ignorant claims about this process. One of the most common objections I hear about the trustworthiness of the Bible goes something like this: "How can you trust the Bible when it's a translation of a translation of a translation? Who knows how much got lost or messed up along the way."

Now, on the surface, this sounds like a reasonable objection. After all, things do get lost when we translate from one language to another, don't they? So if the Bible is the product of a whole string of translations, then wouldn't it stand to reason that we've lost or messed up a lot of what the Bible has to say?

There are two problems with this claim.

First, while things do frequently get mixed up in quick, off-the-cuff translations, this is much less likely to happen in the case of slow, careful translations, especially if there are multiple people who are consulting on the translation project.

I remember teaching in the Ukraine several years ago. Because I don't speak Ukrainian or Russian, I worked with a wonderful translator named Elena. At one point in a lecture, I was making a joke along the lines of "Now, if the bush catches fire and a deep voice speaks to you out of the bush, then you should probably listen." After I said a couple of sentences I paused to let Elena translate, which she did. As I was about to start back up again, though, I noticed that the audience was staring at us with what looked to me like astonishment. Not quite sure what was going on, I turned to Elena and whispered "What did you say?" Elena turned bright red and whispered back, "I said 'Now, if President Bush catches fire...!'" No wonder they were all so shocked!

This is the kind of mistake that can and does happen when translations have to be made quickly, but modern translations of the Bible take years and are very carefully and thoroughly evaluated all along the way by teams of scholars who are evaluating the work step-by-step. In this kind of situation, mistakes of translation are greatly minimized.

The second problem with this attack on the trustworthiness of the Bible is that it is simply untrue. The Bible is not a translation of a translation of a translation. It is simply a one-step translation. Our modern translations are based on the original Hebrew and Greek texts, not on German texts translated from Latin texts translated from Aramaic texts translated from Hebrew texts, etc.

What's The Best Translation Of The Bible?

I am often asked to recommend the "best" English translation of the Bible. Unfortunately, I really don't think there's any such thing. There are two things that make a translation good:

1. It is carefully produced by experts in the original language.

2. It is written with the culture of the modern
   audience in mind.

This second requirement is just as important as the first. As
anyone who has read a novel from 100 years ago can attest,
language changes over time. The English of the 19th century is
not exactly the same as the English of the 21st century. With a
little patience, most modern English-speakers can still understand 19th-century English, but it takes a lot of work. For this
reason, Bible translations need to be updated from time to time,
taking into account changes in language, if they want the contents of God's Word to be understandable.

The King James Version of the Bible was a good translation
in its day, but that was about 400 years ago. Over the last four
centuries, English has changed a lot. Just in case you're not
sure what I mean, check this KJV translation out:

> *But Rabshakeh said, "Hath my master sent me*
> *to thy master and to thee to speak these words?*
> *Hath he not sent me to the men that sit upon*
> *the wall, that they may eat their own dung, and*
> *drink their own piss with you?"*
>
> (Isaiah 36:12)

You know what? If I had ever used that P-word around my
folks, I would have gotten in big trouble. But apparently it was
normal, every-day talk back in King James' day. Language
changes, and it's not just a matter of vocabulary. Sentence
structure, grammar and other basic issues evolve as time goes
by. If translations of the Bible aren't updated from time to
time, God's Word gets harder and harder for people to understand.

But it's not just a matter of language changing across time. It also changes across geography and social location. People in California talk differently than people in Mississippi. Those differences may not be huge, but consider the differences between the way that skaters talk vs. college professors. It's not that one's right and one's wrong; they're just different.

For this reason, there's a great need for different translations of the Bible, even in the same language group, especially if there's a lot of diversity within that group. What communicates well to one age group or social group may not communicate as well to another.

Different translations may also be helpful for different purposes. Personally, I like the New American Standard Bible translation when I'm studying the Bible in English. But I often preach from the New International Version because I think it flows more smoothly and is more natural to listen to for most people. I also use the Message translation at times for teaching, or the English Standard Version for study.

What it all boils down to is: I don't think there is one "best" translation.

However, some translations are better than others. In particular, I think it's a good idea to avoid paraphrases. A paraphrase is an updated version of another translation. The old Living Bible, for instance, started with the King James Version and then modernized the language, but it didn't actually go back to the original Hebrew or Greek. Paraphrases are, in my mind, dangerously close to being a translation of a translation, and the danger of losing important stuff, or just plain mixing it up, is just too great. If you're not sure if a Bible you're considering is a translation or a paraphrase, just look at the preface in the first few pages and you should be able to tell pretty easily.

What About Those Funny Footnotes?

Maybe you've been reading along in a Bible and have come across a verse with an odd little superscripted letter in it, like this:

> *They answered him, "We are Abraham's des-*
> *cendants [b] and have never been slaves of any-*
> *one. How can you say that we shall be set*
> *free?"*
>
> (John 8:33)

When you look at the bottom of the page, you find this:

b 33 Greek seed; also in verse 37

What's going on here? Basically, what you have here is the translators admitting that they're not 100% sure how to translate this passage. Instead of pretending to be certain when they're not, they let you, the reader, in on their process.

There are two general categories of these kinds of notes: translation notes and text notes.

Translation Notes

Translation notes, as in the example above, are simply places where the translators weren't 100% confident that they knew the best way to get across the idea of the verse they were working on. Typically this doesn't mean that they didn't know what the verse said, just that they weren't sure how to best communicate it to their target audience. In the above example, the Greek word would normally be translated as "seed," but the translators knew that when most modern English-speakers hear the word "seed," they think of something different than what the author of the Gospel of John had in mind here. Here, "descendents" seems to get across the idea best. However, there may be some theological reasons why "seed" is actually more accurate in some way, and this was, apparently, an issue that the translation team debated without coming to a completely satisfying conclusion. So what did they do? They translated it the way they thought would communicate best, but also provided a little footnote to let you, the reader, know that they weren't 100% sure that the other option wasn't better.

Text Notes

Text notes are a little more complicated. Maybe you've seen something like this statement, just before the 8th chapter of the Gospel of John:

> [The earliest manuscripts and many other ancient witnesses do not have John 7:53-8:11]

What in the world does *that* mean? In short, it means this: there's a bit of uncertainty about whether the verses of John 7:53-8:11 were actually written by John or were added later by someone else.

To understand this, you need to understand something about the original texts these translations are made from. We don't actually have the original scrolls that the Biblical authors wrote on. The material they first wrote on fell apart a very long time ago, so we don't have access to them. Instead, what we have are copies of them, or, probably more likely, copies of those copies and so on.

Now, while God inspired the original text of the biblical books, we don't have any guarantee in Scripture that each and every copy of those books was superintended by the Holy Spirit in the same way. Which means that, in some cases, the people doing the copies made mistakes. Most of the mistakes were very minor: they skipped a Greek letter here or copied the wrong Hebrew letter there or left out a word or maybe even (very rarely) skipped over a whole line of text.

Most of these kinds of copyist errors are easy to identify because 1) we can tell exactly what kind of mistake happened,[63] and 2) we have other copies of the same text where that mistake wasn't made.

There are scholars who specialize in looking at all the copies we have of biblical texts and comparing them to see if there are differences. These scholars are called *text critics*. Their goal is to make sure that we know exactly what the biblical authors wrote before we translate it into another language. In most cases, this is not a difficult task. The vast majority of the copies agree. However, there are places where there are interesting discrepancies. In such instances, it is the text critics' task to determine what the original, inspired wording was.

To do this, they basically look at two things:

---

[63] For example, if you saw the word "rian" in the sentence "Tut, tut, it looks like rian," you would know that the final word is supposed to be "rain" and that the copyist just flipped the vowels around.

*1. What do the **earliest** manuscripts say?*

This is a pretty basic principle: the closer you are to the source, the less chance there is that something has gotten distorted. If you've ever played the telephone game, you know that the last guy in the chain is much more likely to have a weird version of the original statement than the 2nd or 3rd person in the chain.

Or, put it this way: if the police were investigating an accident, they would want to talk to the people who saw it or to the people who heard it from the eyewitnesses rather than from the guy who heard it from his brother who was talking to this girl who had a cousin who read a blog from a guy who knew this other guy who was there.

For the same reason, when there's a discrepancy among different copies of a Bible verse, we tend to favor the text of the earliest manuscripts.

*2. What do the **majority** of manuscripts say?*

This is another common-sense principle. If you're asking around to find out what happened at an accident scene and find 20 people who say "it was the man in the big pick-up" and only 3 people who say "it was the woman in the little Prius," who do you think actually caused the accident? Further, what if you have good reason to believe that two of the three Prius-blamers actually got their version of the story from the only other Prius-blamer?

Similarly, we tend to favor the text from the majority of manuscripts, especially when we know that the few alternate manuscripts are probably copies of an earlier copy that contains the mistake:

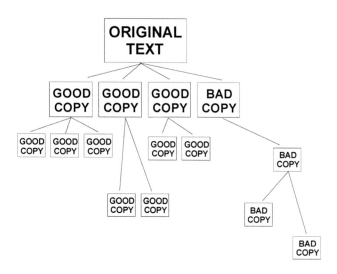

Usually, these two principles are enough to resolve any question about what the original, inspired manuscript said. But on rare occasions, the two principles give out mixed signals. In other words, every now and then, the earliest manuscripts are different from the majority of manuscripts. This suggests that either the earliest manuscripts contain a mistake or that most of the manuscript copies we have were derived from a copy with an error:

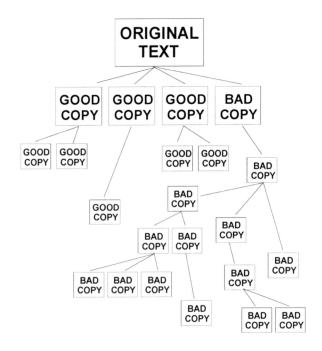

Now keep in mind that a) this doesn't happen very often, and b) in the vast majority of cases where it does happen, the differences are very slight (different spelling of a word, missing letters, etc.).

Still, we want to make sure our Bible is based on the original words of God, so we take each of these differences seriously. When they occur, the first thing text critics ask is "Is there an obvious explanation for the difference?" Usually there is. We can often see exactly how the copyist flipped some letters around or skipped a word because he looked back to the wrong part of the text or simply misread one word for another similar word.

For example, one commonly heard charge against biblical reliability is the fact that in some translations of the Bible, 1

Kings 4:26 and 2 Chronicles 9:25 contain very different numbers for the same thing:

> Solomon had forty thousand stalls for chariot horses, and twelve thousand horses.
>
> (1 Kings 4:26)
>
> Solomon had four thousand stalls for horses and chariots, and twelve thousand horses, which he kept in the chariot cities and also with him in Jerusalem.
>
> (2 Chronicles 9:25)

Obviously these are different numbers, but this is a case where the earliest manuscripts and the majority of the manuscripts have the same discrepancy. However, this is also a case where we can easily explain the copyist error. The Hebrew words for "four" and "forty" look like this:

אַרְבַּעַת   אַרְבָּעִים

If you remember that Hebrew is read from right to left, you'll see how subtle the difference is.[64] What most likely happened was that the copyist glanced at the word, thought he knew what it was and wrote down his mistaken impression. On the basis of this realization, many translations of the Bible

---

[64] Remember, too, that you're looking at a Hebrew typeface rather than a handwritten text. As similar as the two words look when printed in razor-sharp type, imagine how much more similar they might look in fuzzy ink on an ancient papyrus.

correct the obvious copyist error so that you may not even see this supposed "contradiction" in modern Bibles. However, this discrepancy due to a copyist error is often held up as evidence of the Bible's unreliability. But is it evidence of any such thing? No, it is not. Since we can easily tell exactly what happened when someone copied the original inspired text, this is hardly good evidence that the Bible can't be trusted.

In other cases the explanation is that the copyist intentionally changed the spelling of a word or even changed the name of a city to "modernize" it to whatever it was spelled or called in his day. Sometimes the copyists took the liberty of "correcting" what they thought was a grammatical mistake or something. If we can see exactly why a discrepancy occurred between copies we can easily determine what the original text said.

All together, these techniques allow us to reconstruct the original wording of the books of the Bible with tremendous accuracy. Still, there are a very few places where, in spite of our best efforts, we're just not 100% sure we know exactly what the original, inspired text said. When this happens, though, no one tries to cover it up or gloss over it. Instead, this uncertainty is indicated right there in the text of your Bible.

If you flip through your Bible, though, you'll notice that there are only a handful of places where these notes occur, and even where they do, the differences don't amount to anything of substance.

Knowing How God Gave Us the Bible Inspires Confidence in His Word

To me, one of the most encouraging things about the Bible is that God didn't deliver it whole-sale to one guy who we have to put our complete trust in. I mean, I don't know about you, but there's not really anyone besides God that I trust so much that I don't think they could make some serious mistakes. So if one guy told me "Look, here's God's Word!" I'd be a little suspicious. And if this guy told me this book had been copied perfectly for thousands of years without a single error ever showing up, I'd be even more suspicious.

But that's not what happened with the Bible. God gave individual books to individual men, and then God's people as a whole carefully examined those books before agreeing that yes, these books have the fingerprints of God all over them. And, while these books were copied over and over again, God was gracious enough to allow us to have literally thousands of ancient copies of these books so that we can compare them to make sure that we're actually getting the real deal and not a bungled counterfeit.

At the end of the day, we can trust the Bible to tell us the truth about who God is and what He's like. This trust is not a matter of blind faith but merely a reasonable response to the facts.

Understanding
The Bible

Knowing that the Bible is God's Word is one thing. Knowing what God's Word *means* is another thing entirely.

One criticism that skeptics of the Bible often make goes something like this: "People can twist the Bible to say anything they want it to say. Everyone has their own interpretation, so what's the point of reading it?"

There are at least three parts to a good response to this kind of criticism.

1. **Just because the Bible has been twisted by some people to say what they wanted it to say doesn't mean that we can't know what it actually means.**

   There is no doubt that some unscrupulous (and some misguided but otherwise well-intentioned) people have twisted the Bible to say things that it was never intended to say. The Bible has been used over the centuries to justify genocide, slavery and the oppression of women, just to name a few things. But does this mean that the real meaning of the passages used to justify such things cannot be known? Of course not.

   All of us have had something we've said get twisted around by someone else, but how does that happen? Usually it's because that person either took what we said out of context or deliberately misinterpreted what we meant. But does this mean that we're unable to communicate with others most of the time? Of course not.

2. **Just because the Bible has been misinterpreted doesn't mean that it *has* to be misinterpreted. Right interpretation is still possible.**

It is also true that some parts of the Bible have been misunderstood, even though the interpreters weren't trying to justify some personal agenda. For instance, the following verse was taken by many people throughout the centuries as evidence that the sun revolved around the earth:

> *The sun rises and the sun sets, and hurries*
> *back to where it rises.*
>
> (Ecclesiastes 1:5)

We now know that the earth is not the center of the solar system and that this verse should not be taken as a literal scientific statement, but simply as a poetic description of the ways things appear to be, just like when the local news will say that "sunrise will be at 5:52am."

So well-intentioned misunderstandings of the Bible have occurred (and continue to occur). But does this mean that we can't sort out the misunderstandings from the right understandings? Of course not. Right interpretation of the Bible is still possible – it just takes a bit of work sometimes.

3. **Just because some parts of God's Word have been twisted and/or misinterpreted doesn't mean that all parts of the Bible can be twisted or misinterpreted.**

Let's look at two Bible verses and ask a simple question:
Which of these verses is harder to understand?

> *And every woman who prays or prophesies with*
> *her head uncovered dishonors her head – it is*
> *just as though her head were shaved. If a wom-*
> *an does not cover her head, she should have her*
> *hair cut off; and if it is a disgrace for a woman*
> *to have her hair cut or shaved off, she should*
> *cover her head.*
>
> (1 Corinthians 11:5-6)

> *When the water in the skin was gone, she put the*
> *boy under one of the bushes. Then she went off*
> *and sat down nearby, about a bowshot away, for*
> *she thought, "I cannot watch the boy die." And*
> *as she sat there nearby, she began to sob.*
>
> (Genesis 21:15-16)

As anyone can see, the first verse is more difficult to
understand than the second. While all of the words in the
1Co. passage are reasonably familiar, exactly what Paul is
getting at here will be confusing to most modern readers.
But is that true of the second verse? Will anybody read
Gen. 21:15-16 and wonder, "What does it mean that she
'sat down nearby'?" Of course not. My point is quite simple: while there are parts of the Bible that take some work
to understand properly, most of the Bible is immediately
comprehensible to anyone who takes the time to read it.
But what people like to do is take the few difficult-to-

understand passages and act like these are typical of what we find in the Bible. This is simply not true.

Understanding the Bible is really not much different than understanding anything else you read or anything else you hear someone say. There are a few basic rules of interpretation that we use every day without much thinking about them. All we really have to do is apply those rules to what we find in the Bible.

Rule 1 – Ask The Author!

Since the Bible is God's Word, it only makes sense to start your study of God's Word by asking for Him to help you understand it. Now, as we'll discuss below, this doesn't mean that you're off the hook for doing the hard work necessary to interpret God's Word accurately. I'm just saying that it would be stupid to study God's Word without taking advantage of the fact that we have access to the God who gave us that Word. So when you read the Bible, ask God to make you sharp and to help you get out of His Word what He meant for you to find there. Also, ask Him to guard you from misunderstanding or twisting His word.

Now, some people believe that understanding the Bible comes from the Holy Spirit.[65] I don't quite agree, although I do

---

[65] John 16:13 is often cited as evidence for the validity of this belief. There we find that Jesus said that "...the Spirit of truth...will guide you into all the truth...." I believe this is a reference to the role of the Spirit in communicating further revelation (i.e., the New Testament texts) and recollection (i.e., enabling the Apostles to remember Jesus'

believe the Holy Spirit plays a crucial role in our study of God's Word.

It is my opinion, based on both study of God's Word and personal experience, that the Holy Spirit is more concerned with *conviction* than with *exposition*. What I mean is, the Holy Spirit convicts us of how we need to apply God's Word in our lives, but the Holy Spirit does not normally[66] explain to us what each passage of God's Word means.

As evidence of this, I have known non-believers who applied the basic rules of interpretation (that we'll get to shortly) and understand exactly what the Bible says. They just don't believe it's true, and they certainly don't apply it to their lives. On the other hand, I've known Christians who were very confused about parts of the Bible, yet when those parts were explained to them they immediately saw the ways that the meaning of those passages needed to be applied to their lives.

While it might be nice in some ways if the Holy Spirit just told us what the Bible means, there is at least one good reason that I can see why God didn't set it up that way. Think about it: the whole point of the Bible is that it serves as an objective, unchanging standard. But if understanding the Bible could only happen through the Spirit's work, then the Bible wouldn't be objective at all. Suppose one person in church said that the

---

words in a way that allowed them to write the Gospels). I do not think it is a reference to the role of the Holy Spirit in making the Bible comprehensible on an intellectual level.

[66] However, I'm certainly not saying that the Holy Spirit doesn't ever teach us what a passage means. I think this may happen sometimes, but I don't think it's normally what the Holy Spirit does.

Spirit told them that a Bible passage means one thing and another person in church said that the Bible passage means the opposite? The only way they could both be right is if, in fact, the Bible passage in question doesn't actually mean anything at all; in other words, if the meaning were entirely subjective. Of course, we could say that the first person actually heard from the Spirit whereas the second person didn't, but how are we supposed to know who heard from the Holy Spirit and who didn't? Do you see what I'm getting at? The function of the Bible as an objective, unchanging standard requires that its passages actually mean set and settled things that don't change from person to person and from time to time. I believe that's why God didn't set it up so that understanding the Bible comes from the Holy Spirit telling us what each passage means.

However, the Holy Spirit does often tell us how we're each supposed to apply God's Word in our individual lives. The application of truth from Scripture may vary a bit from person to person, but the truth itself will be the same for everyone.

Rule 2 – It Means What The Author *Meant* it to Mean

I vividly remember a creative writing class I took in college. In particular, I remember the day I had to read out loud to the class a poem I had written. When I was done reading it, the professor looked around the room and asked a question I'll never forget: "So, what does this poem mean to you?"

For about ten minutes, I listened to various classmates talk about what the poem "meant." I thought it was like a guessing game; they were trying to figure out what I had intended to say with all the symbolic elements of the poem. But I was wrong.

116 Understanding The Bible

After everyone had shared, the professor started to move on to
the next student's poem. A little surprised I asked, "Don't you
want to know what it means?"

The professor shook his head and said, "What are you talking about? We've already heard what it means?"

"No we haven't," I argued. "I haven't told you."

"But *they've* told me," he gestured to the class. "There's
no set meaning to a poem. It means whatever it means to the
listener."

Honestly, I didn't know what to say to that, so I just
dropped it. Inside, though, I was seething. How could anyone
think that the author of the poem couldn't say what the poem
actually meant? The poem I had written included the line "all
metal, glass and measured lines" which I had written as a reference to science and the sterile way it tends to approach the
study of nature. But one student had said that this line meant
something about finding peace in a landscape of broken hearts.
What? Huh? How could his interpretation be "right" when it
didn't have anything to do with what I intended that line to
communicate?

What this college professor was teaching was an interpretive theory called *Reader Response Criticism*, which argues
that meaning depends on whatever the reader or hearer gets out
of a communication. The major problem with this theory is
that it's self-defeating. Think about it. When my professor
told me that "It means whatever it means to the listener," I was
the listener. Could I have interpreted his statement to mean
that "It means whatever it means to the writer?" Well, according to my professor's theory of interpretation I could! But it
was obvious that he expected me to interpret his statement in
light of what he intended to communicate. In other words,
even though he said that meaning depends on the listener, he

expected me to interpret his statement as though meaning depended on the speaker, which was the opposite of what he was saying!

Does your head hurt trying to sort that out? Don't worry about it. Trying to sort out nonsense often causes headaches. Simply put, you can't even talk about the *Reader Response* theory of interpretation without assuming that what we call the *Authorial Intention* theory of interpretation is actually true. So, you depend on the reality of the very theory of interpretation you're denying in order to talk about the theory you'd like to advocate. It's self-defeating and therefore wrong.[67]

However, a version of the Reader Response theory of interpretation is quite common in Christian circles where people will often "interpret" a verse of the Bible in a way that has no connection to its original meaning. For instance, I know of a woman who was walking through the woods on a piece of property she was thinking of buying. While she walked, she was reading her Bible and came upon the words:

> *He shall build a house for My name, and I will establish the throne of his kingdom forever.*
>
> (2 Samuel 7:13)

---

[67] I have, of course, radically simplified the Reader Response theory of interpretation here, but I stand by the essential accuracy of my critique of it. To be perfectly fair, many advocates of Reader Response interpretation are trying to maintain the value of written texts even when the author's intended meaning for those texts is not clear and the author is no longer accessible for clarification. While I understand this basic impulse, I think that Reader Response Criticism fails on too many logical grounds to be helpful in any meaningful way.

When the woman read this verse, she decided that it "meant" that she should buy that piece of property and build a house there.

Now, I'm not at all opposed to the idea that God speaks directly to us or to the idea that God reveals specific parts of His will for us. However, I am opposed to the idea that passages in the Bible can "mean" things that have nothing to do with their original context or the original intention of their authors. The prevalence of this kind of "interpretation" in the Church is dangerous because it undermines the entire basis of responsible biblical interpretation, and because it often leads people to "trust in the Lord" regarding promises that He has never made!

The alternative theory of interpretation is the one we use every day: *Authorial Intention.* This theory simply says that a statement means whatever the author of that statement intended to communicate.

Now, what someone *intends* to communicate and what someone else actually *understands* may not be the same thing. There may be several reasons for this: the listener may not be listening carefully, the speaker might not do a very good job of communicating what he or she is trying to get across, etc. When this happens, we say that there has been a misunderstanding. Regardless of whose fault the misunderstanding is, though, the whole idea of a misunderstanding assumes the Authorial Intent theory of interpretation: a statement has been rightly interpreted when the listener understands what the speaker intended to communicate.

So as we read the Bible, our goal is simple: to understand what the author of the passage we're reading was intending to communicate. Because every part of the Bible has two authors (God and His human servant), we might say that the goal of biblical interpretation is to understand what the A(a)uthor intended to communicate.

Rule 3 – Context, Context, Context

The most important principle to keep in mind as we seek to understand what the A(a)uthor of a biblical passage intended to communicate is this: *context reveals meaning.* Notice that I didn't say that context determines meaning, because as we've already seen, the meaning of a passage is determined by the A(a)uthor's intention. But this meaning is most often made clear to us when we keep in mind the context of that passage. Therefore, *context reveals meaning.*

What is context? Context is just the stuff that surrounds a passage we're reading. To illustrate the importance of context, and what can happen when we ignore it, consider the following text:

> *The inhabitants of the earth will celebrate by sending each other gifts...*
> (Revelation 11:10)

One of my students once showed me a Christmas card he had received with this verse printed on it. It was easily the worst Christmas card I have ever come across. Why? Here, read the rest of this passage *in context*:

> *And I will give power to my two witnesses, and they will prophesy for 1,260 days, clothed in sackcloth." These are the two olive trees and the two lampstands that stand before the Lord of the earth. If anyone tries to harm*

them, fire comes from their mouths and devours their enemies. This is how anyone who wants to harm them must die. These men have power to shut up the sky so that it will not rain during the time they are prophesying; and they have power to turn the waters into blood and to strike the earth with every kind of plague as often as they want. Now when they have finished their testimony, the beast that comes up from the Abyss will attack them, and overpower and kill them. Their bodies will lie in the street of the great city, which is figuratively called Sodom and Egypt, where also their Lord was crucified. For three and a half days men from every people, tribe, language and nation will gaze on their bodies and refuse them burial. <u>The inhabitants of the earth will</u> gloat over them and will <u>celebrate by sending each other gifts,</u> because these two prophets had tormented those who live on the earth.

(Revelation 11:3-10)

When we read verse Rev. 11:10 in its entirety and in context – with all the surrounding material – it's quite obvious that this is not a Christmas sentiment. Instead, it's a prophecy about how evil people will celebrate when God's witnesses are dead and rotting in the street! Merry Christmas! Not!

Context reveals meaning by clarifying all kinds of things. As in the case above, it sometimes clarifies the *significance* of something.

Context can also reveal meaning by clarifying what individual words mean. Imagine that you came across the following sentence, all by itself:

Today was cool.

The meaning of "today" is probably not going to be a matter of any serious debate among interpreters, and everyone knows what "was" means, but "cool" is another matter, isn't it? "Cool" could mean "having a low temperature" or it could be a synonym for "great, awesome, fun, etc." But which is it? Without context, there's really no way to be sure what the author of this sentence intended.

Imagine, however, that this sentence was followed by another sentence that read:

So I collected extra firewood to make ready for a difficult evening.

Now the meaning of "cool" is perfectly clear. Context can be more than just the surrounding words, though. Context is literally everything that surrounds a passage, including the characteristics of the author and the historical period in which the passage was written. If you knew, for instance that "today was cool" was a sentence from a 14-year-old girl's diary, you probably wouldn't assume it was an observation about the day's temperature fluctuations. On the other hand, if it was found in a 17th-century meteorologist's logbook, it probably isn't a synonym for "wicked sweet." All of these kinds of things, and more, are part of the context of a passage which reveals its meaning.

When we're reading a passage and aren't quite sure what it means, I believe there are eight basic kinds of context that we should pay attention to:

1. Immediate Literary Context
2. Genre Context
3. Larger Literary Context
4. Book Context
5. Authorial Context
6. Testament Context
7. Whole Bible Context
8. Historical/Cultural Context

1. Immediate Literary Context

What insight do we gain by looking at the other words and sentences that surround the passage?

The Gospel of Matthew tells us that:

> *In those days John the Baptist came, preaching*
> *in the Desert of Judea and saying, "Repent, for*
> *the kingdom of heaven is near."*
> (Matthew 3:1-2)

What did he mean when he said that the kingdom of heaven was "near"? If we continue reading the passage, this is clarified:

*Then Jesus came from Galilee to the Jordan to
be baptized by John. But John tried to deter
him, saying, "I need to be baptized by you, and
do you come to me?" Jesus replied, "Let it be
so now; it is proper for us to do this to fulfill
all righteousness." Then John consented. As
soon as Jesus was baptized, he went up out of
the water. At that moment heaven was opened,
and he saw the Spirit of God descending like a
dove and lighting on him. And a voice from
heaven said, "This is my Son, whom I love;
with him I am well pleased."*

(Matthew 3:13-17)

Once we consider the rest of the immediate literary context, it becomes obvious that John the Baptist was saying that
the kingdom of heaven was "near" because Jesus was about to
begin his ministry. In the person of Jesus, the kingdom of heaven has arrived. It is no longer a distant and remote thing but a
here-and-now reality.

2. Genre Context

What type of literature is the passage and how does that af-
fect our interpretation of it?

Jesus often spoke using vivid language designed to get his
listeners' attention and force them to consider his point carefully. For instance:

*If your hand causes you to sin, cut it off. It is
better for you to enter life maimed than with*

*two hands to go into hell, where the fire never
goes out.*

(Mark 9:43)

*If your right eye causes you to sin, gouge it out
and throw it away. It is better for you to lose
one part of your body than for your whole
body to be thrown into hell.*

(Matthew 5:29)

Did Jesus mean this literary? Should we be cutting off
body parts every time they're involved in sin of some kind?
Doubtful, since other parts of the Bible say that everyone sins,
but God doesn't give any indication that everyone is supposed
to be walking around with self-inflicted amputations.

More importantly, Jesus' statements here are examples of
poetic speech. Poetic speech often involves hyperbole: exag-
gerations intended to make a point. When we recognize this,
we understand that a) we're not supposed to be maiming ourselves when we sin, but that b) sin is very serious business and
we can't take it lightly. Understanding the genre context of
these verses makes this meaning clear.

3. Larger Literary Context

Most biblical books have distinct sections (often indicated
by chapter numbers). What themes are being addressed in this
section of the book and how does that help us understand this
particular passage?

The Gospel of John contains an interesting statement that
often puzzles readers. In a conversation with a man named
Nicodemus, Jesus said this:

*I tell you the truth, no one can enter the king-
dom of God unless he is born of water and the
Spirit.*

(John 3:5)

The rest of the Gospel of John explains what it means to be born of the Spirit, but what does it mean to be born of water? Several options have been suggested. Some have thought that it means the water that "breaks" just before a baby is born. Others have thought that it is a reference to the water of baptism, meaning that to be saved you have to be baptized first. A number of other suggestions have been made as well. When we consider the larger literary context of this passage, however, Jesus' meaning is clear.

This verse is part of a section of the Gospel of John that focuses on the old ways (apart from Jesus) and the new way (by faith in Jesus). This section begins in chapter 2 and runs through to the end of chapter 4. Once we recognize this theme in this section, it seems clear that Jesus was using "water" in John 3:5 as a reference to the "old" way of being born; in other words, as a reference to physical birth, as contrasted with the spiritual birth that he offers and which is accomplished by the Holy Spirit. Understanding the larger literary context reveals the intended meaning.

4. Book Context

What themes does this whole book of the Bible address, and how does that help us understand this particular passage?

The book of Ephesians has a verse that may be the source of confusion to many readers if they don't understand the themes of that book as a whole:

And God raised us up with Christ and seated us with him in the heavenly realms in Christ Jesus...

(Ephesians 2:6)

What does it mean for us to be "seated in the heavenly realms"? In short, it means that we have authority (because of our faith in Jesus) over the evil spirits who inhabit the heavenly realms. That this is Paul's intended meaning becomes clear when we see that spiritual warfare (i.e., our battle against evil spirits) is a central theme of the book of Ephesians. Reading the whole book carefully will reveal several key passages related to this theme, the most famous of which is probably:

Finally, be strong in the Lord and in his mighty power. Put on the full armor of God so that you can take your stand against the devil's schemes. For our struggle is not against flesh and blood, but against the rulers, against the authorities, against the powers of this dark world and against the spiritual forces of evil in the heavenly realms.

(Ephesians 6:10-12)

Most books of the Bible are not random collections of thoughts. There is usually a clear progression of thought, often revolving around a few key themes. Recognizing those themes will often shed light on particular passages within the book.

5. Authorial Context

Has the author of this book written other books? Does he tend to use particular words in certain ways? Are there other places where he has addressed related issues that will help us understand this passage?

I hate to take potshots at a popular sermon topic, but I'm going to anyway. At the end of the Gospel of John there's a passage that says this:

> *So when they had finished breakfast, Jesus said to Simon Peter, "Simon, son of John, do you love Me more than these?" He said to Him, "Yes, Lord; You know that I love You." He said to him, "Tend My lambs." He said to him again a second time, "Simon, son of John, do you love Me?" He said to Him, "Yes, Lord; You know that I love You." He said to him, "Shepherd My sheep." He said to him the third time, "Simon, son of John, do you love Me?" Peter was grieved because He said to him the third time, "Do you love Me?" And he said to Him, "Lord, You know all things; You know that I love You." Jesus said to him, "Tend My sheep.*
>
> (John 21:15-17)

The reason this passage is so popular is because it gives preachers a chance to show off a little bit. See, the Greek language has several words for "love": *agape, philea, storge* and *eros.* Technically, each of these words has slightly different meanings. *Agape*, for instance, often means self-giving love whereas *philea* often means friendship type love. What's interesting is that according to the passage above, Jesus asked Peter if he *agape-ed* him and Peter kept responding that he *phileo-ed* Jesus. The typical sermon on this passage says that Jesus had to ask Peter three times if he loved him because Peter refused to respond with the right love-word: Peter was only willing to indicate friendship with Jesus, not self-sacrificing love.

This makes for a great sermon, but unfortunately it's bad interpretation. First, it ignores the larger literary context. Remember what Peter had just done three times? Right, he denied Jesus. It is far more likely that Jesus asked him this question three times because of the three denials. Note that at the end of each of the three interchanges, Jesus gave Peter a job to do. Jesus was essentially re-instating Peter in spite of his three failures, telling Peter that Jesus still had a place for him in the Kingdom.

But beyond the larger literary context, there is something else that points towards this interpretation: the way John uses the Greek words for love. Because John wrote several books (The Gospel of John, 1 John, 2 John, 3 John and Revelation) and because John wrote frequently of love, we have several books of his in which to observe how he uses these two Greek words, *agape* and *philea*. As it turns out, John used *agape* and *philea* as synonyms for the same thing. In other words, he doesn't seem to have made the distinction between *agape* as sacrificial love and *philea* as friendship love.

When preachers teach on this passage and make this big distinction between the *agape* and *philea*, they usually say that *agape* is divine love whereas *philea* is inferior human love.

But it's clear that John doesn't use the two words that way. For instance, John says:

> *This is the judgment, that the Light has come into the world, and men <u>loved</u> the darkness rather than the Light, for their deeds were evil.*
>
> (John 3:19)

The Greek word translated as "love" in this verse is *agape*. So is John saying that men self-sacrificially loved darkness? That doesn't really make any sense. Moreover, while John does sometimes say that God *agape-s* us, he also says that God *phileo-s* us:

> *Those whom I <u>love,</u> I reprove and discipline; therefore be zealous and repent.*
>
> (Revelation 3:19)

Here the Greek word translated as "love" is *philea*. Does this mean that God only has the inferior friendship kind of love for His people? Of course not.

The point is simply that John uses *agape* and *philea* as synonyms for "love" without maintaining any kind of meaningful distinction between the Greek terms. This knowledge, obtained by looking at other books written by John, helps us to avoid interpretive mistakes when looking at particular passages he's written.

6. Testament Context

Does the Old or the New Testament (depending on where the passage occurs) have other passages dealing with related themes and issues? How does seeing the way the whole Testament treats this issue help us understand the passage?

If you do a word search on the term "faith" in the Bible you'll find an interesting thing: the word "faith" is quite rare in the Old Testament but extremely common in the New Testament. In the O.T., "faith" often refers to keeping one's promises:

> *If she does not please the master who has selected her for himself, he must let her be redeemed. He has no right to sell her to foreigners, because he has broken faith with her.*
>
> (Exodus 21:8)

In the New Testament, however, it typically means something more like "placing one's trust in something or someone":

> *Jesus stepped into a boat, crossed over and came to his own town. Some men brought to him a paralytic, lying on a mat. When Jesus saw their <u>faith</u>, he said to the paralytic, "Take heart, son; your sins are forgiven."*
>
> (Matthew 9:1-2)

> *Later Jesus appeared to the Eleven as they were eating; he rebuked them for their lack of <u>faith</u> and their stubborn refusal to believe those who had seen him after he had risen.*
>
> (Mark 16:14)

If you're reading a passage that has the word "faith" in it, looking at which Testament the passage is part of will help you understand it.

7. Whole Bible Context

Are there passages in other parts of the Bible where this issue, or a related one, is discussed? How does reading about this issue in other parts of the Bible help us understand this passage?

Biblical writers, especially the New Testament ones, often assumed that their readers were familiar with the rest of Scripture. Consequently, they sometimes didn't explain things that might be confusing to some readers. For instance, imagine that you had no church background and had never read the Bible and you came across this passage:

> *Jesus sent Peter and John, saying, "Go and make preparations for us to eat the Passover."*
> (Luke 22:8)

What, you might ask, is a "Passover"? Is it some kind of pastry? How complicated can eating it, whatever it is, be? Why do they have to make preparations before eating it? Is it some kind of poison that you have to build up an immunity for?

These would be natural questions if you had never heard of Passover before. But if you had read Exodus, you would have known that the Passover was a special, ritualistic meal by which the Jewish people celebrated their release from slavery in Egypt. The New Testament writers didn't explain this because they assumed everyone knew what the Passover celebration was. Without a knowledge of the whole Bible context, however, modern readers might be very confused about references to Passover in the New Testament.

8. Historical/Cultural Context

Are there things that I need to understand about the original culture in which this passage was written, or about the audience it was written to, that will help me understand this passage?

In some ways, reading the Bible is a little bit like reading someone else's mail. If you don't know anything about the person it was written to, there may be parts of it that are confusing. While God inspired the Bible for you – and for all of His people throughout history – it wasn't directly written to you. Each book of the Bible was directly written to particular groups of people in particular circumstances. Sometimes, knowing something about those circumstances or the culture of the people the book was originally written to will help us understand what the Bible means.

Several of the examples about context above, such as the bit about the Passover, really boil down to understanding something about the cultural and historical context of the original audience. Often these kinds of things can be found out from the Bible itself, but sometimes it is helpful to get a bit more background.

As an example, consider this famous passage from the book of Revelation:

"To the angel of the church in Laodicea write:
These are the words of the Amen, the faithful

*and true witness, the ruler of God's creation. I
know your deeds, that you are neither cold nor
hot. I wish you were either one or the other!
So, because you are lukewarm – neither hot
nor cold – I am about to spit you out of my
mouth."*

(Revelation 3:14-16)

Sometimes people read this passage and assume that "hot" means "passionate about God" (as in "on fire for the Lord") and that "cold" means "not really caring much about God at all." Now, this might make for an inspiring sermon, but is it what God intended to say in this passage? Right away, this interpretation ought to cause some red flags to go up because God says here that He wishes people were either hot or cold. Does it really make sense that God wants people to totally not care about Him at all instead of just kind-of caring about Him? I mean, isn't it better to give *some* thought to what God wants than to not care about Him at all?

But what else could this mean? Well, actually, with a little bit of cultural/historical context, this passage makes perfect sense. See, the city of Laodicea had no usable water supply, so they piped their water in via aqueducts.[68] The source of this water was either hot springs or cool mountain pools, but by the time the water reached Laodicea, the hot water had cooled off and the cool water had warmed up. Now, hot water has some important uses: it's great for washing things or healing aching muscles. Cool water, on the other hand, is great to drink. It

---

[68] Johnson, "Revelation", 456-457.

refreshes the body. But lukewarm water? It's not really good for cleansing or healing, and it's not very refreshing to drink. This is what Jesus is referring to in this passage from Revelation: the Christians in Laodicea were neither zealous about healing those who were hurt and helping them clean up their lives, nor were they encouraging and refreshing to those who had been beat up by their struggles in life. In other words, this passage isn't really about how the Christians there felt about God, but about how they treated each other. This is a great example of how knowing the historical/cultural background of a passage can help us understand what the A(a)uthor intended to say.

These kinds of context are not all equally helpful in studying a given passage. In fact, for most passages, just paying attention to the first one, the immediate literary context, is enough to make the meaning clear. Sometimes, however, the immediate literary context isn't quite enough to clear up questions that we may have, so we have to expand the context we're considering a bit. In general, I think it's safe to say that the kinds of context above are listed in order of their initial significance. So, when you think about what a passage means, you can usually start by looking at the immediate literary context and gradually move outward from that if questions still remain:

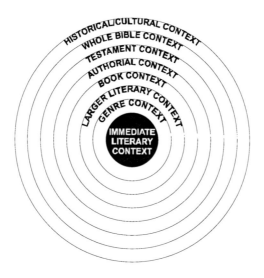

Rule 4 – Don't Swim Alone

It has sometimes been said that the Bible contains shallows where a mouse can wade and depths where an elephant can drown.[69] Don't dive into the deep parts alone!

All I really mean is this: responsible Biblical interpretation is best done in community, alongside other Christians who can help us avoid making interpretive mistakes. Most of the misunderstandings and outright twistings of Scripture that have occurred over the centuries have been because someone

---

[69] In other words, the Bible has easy-to-understand parts and hard-to-understand parts.

thought they were too smart to see what others thought about an interpretation.

God has not called us to live as Christians alone, so we shouldn't be studying His Word alone, either.

Now, when I say that we should study God's word alongside others, I don't necessarily mean that we can't do individual Bible study or that we should only read the Bible in groups. No, what I mean is that we should always make sure that our understanding of the Bible is consistent with what other followers of Christ have understood it to say. There are several ways to do this:

Get Involved With A Church That Takes Bible-Teaching Seriously

This is the most basic requirement for responsible Bible interpretation: surround yourself with people who take the Bible seriously and seek to both understand what it says and obey its teachings. The absolute best way to find these people is to be active in a church made up of these kinds of people.

Join a Small-Group Bible Study

A small group of people who are studying the Bible together and sharing their insights and understanding is a great way to go deeper into God's Word.

Bounce Your Understandings Off A Trusted Mentor

It's always great to have people in your life who know more than you do. They're great resources for advice, encouragement and, sometimes, correction. Bouncing your understanding of passages from the Bible off of these mentors is important because they can help make sure you're not misunderstanding something or, worse, twisting God's Word to say something that God never meant to say.

For what it's worth, I have a Ph.D. in Biblical Studies, but I also have a great friend and mentor whose general judgment and Bible knowledge I trust. I'm constantly calling him up and saying, "So, I've been looking at this passage and it seems to me that God is saying..." It's just my way of making sure I'm not going off on some crazy wild-goose chase as I seek to understand what God is saying to me through His Word.

Make Use Of Bible-Study Tools

There are a lot of great resources out there to help you understand the Bible. When you find yourself not quite sure of what a passage of the Bible means, these are great tools to have around. Here's a quick run-down of the basic tools:

- *Study Bibles*
  Study Bibles are simply Bibles with helpful notes and information, usually in the margins or at the bottom of each page. I highly recommend that everyone who is serious about understanding God's Word have a study Bible that they use regularly.

- *Commentaries*
  Commentaries are books that go in-depth into the historical-cultural background of Bible books and, often, give insight into the original language be-

hind the translation. Commentaries help you work through various issues to help you understand what each passage in the Bible book means.

- *Dictionaries*
  You probably know what dictionaries are: they give you definitions of words. A good English dictionary can be very helpful when studying the Bible because sometimes the translations use words that aren't familiar to us from every-day life. There are also Bible dictionaries that give more in-depth information about the people, places and concepts in the Bible.

- *Topical Books*
  Some issues that arise from reading the Bible require more thorough explanations than can be given in notes at the bottom of a page or even in the extended treatment of a commentary. Often these issues are treated in full-length books. If, for instance, you want to understand more about the way the sacrificial system of the O.T. relates to the faith in Jesus of the N.T., there are detailed examinations available of precisely that issue.

- *Concordances*
  Concordances are books that give every word in the Bible and then tell you every place in the Bible where that word occurs. This can be helpful for things like looking at how certain words are used by particular authors. Each concordance is keyed to a particular Bible translation so, for instance,

you can get a concordance of the NIV or the KJV. Concordances are currently becoming less and less popular as they are replaced by Bible software (see next).

- *Bible Study Software*
  Bible study software allows you to not only read the Bible on digital devices, but also allows you to search for words and phrases, and even access commentaries and dictionaries that apply to each verse you're looking at. Some of these programs can even be accessed online for free (though in limited form).

Digging Deeper Into Biblical Interpretation

The various things discussed in this chapter are really only the tip of the iceberg. I believe the rules I've outlined here and the basic ideas that I've explained will go a long way towards helping you understand the Bible. After all, God didn't make the Bible difficult to comprehend because He wanted you to understand it.

However, having said that, I also need to let you know that we've only scratched the surface here. This book is, in no way, a thorough examination of all the issues related to responsible biblical interpretation.

When you're ready to go deeper, your best bet is to pick up a full-length book on something called *hermeneutics*. Hermeneutics is the study of interpretation, and a good book on biblical hermeneutics will be a great asset to you as you study God's Word. Such books will explore in-depth issues like how to know when the Bible intends something to be understood figuratively and when it is intended to be understood literally, or how to understand the ways that lines of Hebrew poetry relate to each other.

If you're interested in such a book, I have two recommendations for you:

Introduction to Biblical Interpretation by William Klein, Craig Blomberg and Robert Hubbard (Dallas: Word Publishing, 1993).

The Hermeneutical Spiral: A Comprehensive Introduction to Biblical Interpretation by Grant R Osborne (Downers Grove: Intervarsity Press, 2006).

Defending The Bible

We have already addressed several of the most commonly voiced skepticisms about the Bible, but there are several other things that remain to be said.

It is worth noting again here that our confidence in the Bible is crucial on several levels. First, if we can trust the Bible then we can trust what it says about Jesus and, in turn, we can trust what it says about God. In that sense, our confidence in the Bible is personally important. Second, if we can trust the Bible then we can be confident when we share our faith with others. In that sense, our confidence in the Bible is evangelistically important. Without confidence in the Bible we can't be confident about sharing our faith or even about living it out consistently. Therefore, our ability to defend the Bible is both personally and culturally important.

What I would like to do in the next few pages is give you a way of thinking about defending the Bible that will enable you to address specific issues as you encounter them. Rather than trying to give you an encyclopedia of answers to common objections, I want to provide a model that can be applied to both common objections and to new objections that will surface in coming years.

Leveling The Playing Field

Perhaps the simplest way to defend the Bible against the attacks of modern skepticism is to insist on a level playing field for the conversation. What I mean is, modern skepticism of the Bible often holds the Bible to a different standard than is applied to other written works. When the playing field is leveled, however, and the reliability of the Bible is evaluated according to common standards, a great many of the objections simply disappear.

Approximations

One place where different standards seem to be applied to the Bible frequently is that of approximations or round numbers. For instance, I have been told several times that the Bible is historically inaccurate because it uses round numbers. For example:

> *So the Philistines fought, and the Israelites were defeated and every man fled to his tent. The slaughter was very great; Israel lost thirty thousand foot soldiers.*
>
> (1 Samuel 4:10)

It might sound ridiculous to you, but I've actually heard people say that this statement is proof of the Bible's inaccuracy. "Are you trying to tell me," they say, "that we're supposed to believe that people died in perfectly round numbers?!"

"Of course not!" I respond, "But are you trying to tell me that saying 30,000 instead of 28,723 is an 'error'?"

The reality is that most accounts, biblical or otherwise, use round numbers, usually because precise numbers simply aren't available. We don't know, for instance, exactly how many Jewish people were killed during the Holocaust, but no-one says that the normal figure, six million, is wrong simply because it's rounded. Some people might object that this number is too high, but the argument is about whether or not six million is a good approximation, not whether the number is wrong *because* it's been rounded.

Of course, round numbers and approximations can be wrong. If, in the battle described in 1 Sa. 4, the precise death-toll was 21,458, thirty thousand would simply be an inaccurate approximation. In that case, twenty thousand would be an accurate approximation, but rounding up to thirty thousand would simply be wrong. In other words, allowing for round numbers doesn't mean that accuracy no longer counts. There are still rules that must be followed when using round numbers, but the use of round numbers themselves is not proof of inaccuracy.

This is a good example of the kind of thing I mean when I say that part of defending the Bible is insisting on a level playing field. Round numbers are expected in many kinds of reports, especially ancient ones, and they do not cause people to question the reliability of those reports. If we allow round numbers in other reports we shouldn't insist on a different standard of evaluation when it comes to the Bible.

Getting The "Gist" vs. Verbatim Transcriptions

On a related note, ancient texts – and many modern ones as well – are considered to be perfectly reliable when they accurately report the gist of what someone says rather than reproducing a verbatim transcription of each and every word that was spoken. Thus, for example, if someone were to report that "Tim said he was going out to dinner with Rob and some other friends," this would be considered an accurate quote even though Tim actually said, "I'm going out to dinner with Rob, Nicole, Danny and Whitney." No-one in this instance would say that the report was inaccurate because the report of Tim's statement captured the "gist," even though it didn't reproduce every word or even every detail. We would, of course, say that one report was more specific than another, but as in the case of round numbers and approximations as well, specificity and accuracy aren't the same thing.

We are happy with this kind of summation even in the modern world where recording devices often make it possible to capture someone's words exactly so that they can later by typed up in a perfect word-for-word reproduction. If we accept this sort of thing now, how much more acceptable or expected was it in the ancient world where the human memory was the only "recording" device available? In all kinds of ancient literature where someone's words are recorded, it is expected that the writers summarized the speech rather than trying to get every word right. In other words, when we read an ancient historian's report of a speech by Socrates or a Roman emperor, their report is considered accurate as long as it does not contain any errors of content. It doesn't have to be a verbatim, word-for-word transcription to be considered a reliable account of the speech. This is simply common sense, yet this basic, common-sense principle is often not applied to the Bible.

For example, one objection to the reliability of the Bible that I've heard many times is the charge that the Gospel writers made mistakes in quoting Jesus' teaching. In Matthew 6:22-23 and Luke 11:34-36, for instance, both Gospel writers are clearly reporting the same teaching from Jesus, but with some slight differences:

> *The eye is the lamp of the body. If your eyes are good, your whole body will be full of light. But if your eyes are bad, your whole body will be full of darkness...*
>
> (Matthew 6:22-23)

*Your eye is the lamp of your body. When your
eyes are good, your whole body also is full of
light. But when they are bad, your body also is
full of darkness.*

(Luke 11:34-35)

Though there is no difference of substance between these
two reports of Jesus' teaching, skeptics use this sort of thing to
argue that the Bible is not reliable. This is simply ridiculous;
the standards that we use to assess the Bible's reliability
shouldn't be different than those we use to assess other sources;
if we're happy with summations or "getting the gist" in other
texts, we should be happy with summations in the Bible.

What this boils down to is the simple idea that when we
encounter people who are skeptical about the reliability of the
Bible, one of the first things we need to do is find out what
standards they are using to evaluate the Bible and then make
sure those standards are *fair*, or can be meaningfully applied to
other things. If an unrealistic standard is being applied, then
getting people to recognize this is the first step in defending the
reliability of the Bible.

Dates & Dating

One area in which people are often skeptical of the Bible
relates to dates. A typical argument will often go something
like this: *the Bible isn't reliable because it says that event X
happened on date Y but it actually happened on date Z.*

When we encounter this kind of objection, there are two
questions we need to ask. First, we need to ask if the Bible

actually says that the event happened on date Y. Second, we need to ask if the event really happened on date Z.

For example, many people object to the reliability of the Bible because:

> "The Bible says the earth was created about 6,000 years ago but we know that it actually came into existence 4 billion years ago."

Let's explore this objection in light of the two questions above. First, does the Bible really say that the earth was created about 6,000 years ago? I don't think so. I think the Bible *might* say that the earth was created about 6,000 years ago, (in other words, that this is one possible interpretation) but I don't have any confidence at all that this is really what the Bible claims (in other words, I'm not at all sure that this is the interpretation that the A(a)uthor of Genesis intended). It is quite possible that the "days" of Genesis 1 are actually extended periods of time during which God created particular kinds of things.[70] When His creation of those things came to an end, the "day" was over and the next one began. This interpretation has been held by many Bible-believing Christians for

---

[70] The Hebrew word "yom" which is translated as "day" can mean a 24-hour period or a period of indeterminate length, defined only by the kind of activity that is going on. Isaiah 13:6, for instance, says this: "Wail, for the day of the LORD is near; it will come like destruction from the Almighty." Here, the "day of the Lord" is a reference to a future period of judgment which other prophetic texts in the Bible make clear will be more than a single 24-hour period during which God's judgment is poured out on the evil in our world.

centuries, long before evolutionary theory was introduced. It has been held because there are important linguistic and interpretive issues that have to be considered as we read Genesis 1. Now, this doesn't mean that the "days" of Genesis are definitely long periods of time, but it does mean that we can't say with certainty that "the Bible says the earth was created 6,000 years ago." This is simply not something we know for certain.

But what about the second question? Do we actually know that the earth came into existence 4 billion years ago? Again, I'm not at all sure that this is the case. First, this idea of the earth's age is largely based on presupposition (things that people believe before looking at the evidence). Since evolutionary theory has come to dominate our scientific thinking, it has had a profound influence on fields of science besides biology. In this case, the influence works like this: for evolution to happen, you need a LOT of time, therefore life must have been around on earth for a long time, and therefore the earth itself must have been around for a long time. With this kind of thinking, people begin to interpret the data in light of their expectations and suddenly the dominant theory is that the earth is 4 billion years old. Now, this is not to say that there is no evidence that the earth is relatively old. Radiometric dating, for instance, does suggest that the earth is quite old. However, there are some significant weaknesses in the practice of radiometric dating and the results are not always consistent with an old-earth theory. These results are often thrown out as unreliable because they don't fit the currently accepted theory of the earth's age. In the same way, anomalous evidence like the relatively rapid rate of decay of the earth's magnetic field, the small amount of dust build-up on the moon, and other things of a similar nature suggest that the earth may not be as old as is currently thought. But this is ignored simply because it doesn't fit what we expect to find.

Now, I'm not saying that the earth is *not* 4 billion years old. As I said before, I think it's quite possible that Genesis speaks of an earth that has been around for a long time (although I do not believe in evolution as an explanation for the life that inhabits the earth), so I'm not presuppositionally opposed to an old earth. All I'm saying is that the claim that the Bible is unreliable because it says 6,000-year-old-earth when it fact it's a 4-billion-year-old earth is weak. First, it's not at all clear that the Bible says 6,000 years, and second, it is far from a certain fact that the earth is actually 4 billion years old.

A similar kind of thing occurs when we deal with more traditional historical events. The Bible, for instance, gives three pieces of evidence related to Jesus' birth:

1. He was born during a census ordered by the Roman emperor Augustus.
2. He was born during the Syrian reign of the Roman governor Quirinius.
3. He was born during the reign of the Jewish ruler Herod the Great.

Some skeptics charge that the Bible is historically unreliable at this point because the only Roman-Empire-wide census we know about while Quirinius was governor of Syria occurred in 6-7 A.D., some ten years after the supposed birth of Christ.[71] How do we respond to this?

---

[71] As we will see below, contrary to popular thinking, Jesus was most likely born between 8-4 B.C.

First, the Biblical evidence is fairly straightforward, with one important exception. The Greek word translated as "governor" (Luke 1:2) was used for a fairly wide range of administrative duties within the Roman government and could therefore be referring to a tour of duty Quirinius had in Syria years before he assumed the formal role of governor over the region. Second, we do know of an empire-wide census taken in 8 B.C., but does this help? It might. There are at least two things to keep in mind:

1. Jesus was born a bit earlier than we typically think. Most people assume that he was born in 1 A.D., but this is not correct. In the 6th century A.D. when our current calendar was adopted, some rather complicated mathematical calculations resulted in a calendar which misdated Jesus' birth by several years. Herod the Great, who tried to kill the baby Jesus, is known to have died in what we call 4 B.C., and since he didn't order the infanticide from his grave, we have to date Jesus' birth sometime earlier than 4 B.C. Since Herod wanted to kill all babies 2 years and younger, this would mean that Jesus would not likely have been born any later than 6 B.C., and may in fact have been born a year or two earlier. This alone might put the biblical data in perfect alignment with the empire-wide census of 8 B.C.

2. The 8 B.C. census may have occurred a bit later than 8 B.C., possibly in 7 or even early 6 B.C., which would make aligning the biblical data with the other known historical data even easier.

The problem with dating ancient events is that they didn't use our calendar. In fact, different nations used entirely different calendars. The Romans, for instance, sometimes counted years based on when they believed the city of Rome had been founded. So, what we call 1-100 A.D., they called 754-854. The Jews, assuming that the days of Genesis 1 were 24-hour periods and estimating the years since then based on their reconciliation of the various genealogies in the Bible, called the same period 3760-3860.

More often, however, people used relative dating systems based on when rulers came into power. Luke, for instance, dates the beginning of John the Baptist's ministry to "the fifteenth year of the reign of Tiberius Caesar" (Luke 3:1). As if this weren't complicated enough, there's an additional problem: what counts as the first year of a ruler's reign? If (using our calendar) the U.S. president took office in September, would you call that partial year his first year or start counting his first year only in January when he will be able to serve a full year? I'm sure you see the problem. Then there's the problem of the fact that the Roman calendar and the Jewish calendar started at different times of the year![72]

All in all, saying that a particular ancient event happened on a specific year is quite difficult. Normally, the best we can do is give a time-frame. This doesn't mean that we have no idea when something happened, only that we can't be too precise or assume too much certainty in our dating of events.

So, in the case above, it is quite likely that Jesus was born around 7 B.C., right at the time of a known empire-wide cen-

---

[72] The Jewish year begins in our March-April time period.

sus, and apparently during a time when Quirinius was in Syria in some administrative capacity.

Of course, if you've already decided that the Bible is historically faulty, you may look at this explanation and say, "You're really reaching," but the fact is that this sort of working through the complex bits of evidence is something that is done constantly in the case of *all* historical reports. What's really interesting is this: when we come across an ancient report that gives some evidence for an event that doesn't fit with our present understanding of ancient history, we don't automatically dismiss the report as being mistaken. Instead, we carefully consider all the evidence to make sure we hadn't previously misinterpreted the other bits of evidence we had. Even more interestingly, when we can't seem to make the new evidence fit our previous theories, we often become a bit agnostic, saying that new evidence has called into question our previous historical theories and becoming reluctant to be dogmatic about what happened and when.

But do the skeptics treat the Bible the same way? No, they don't. Rather than saying "The Bible presents some evidence that causes us to re-consider our previous theories about historical events," they say "We know that the Bible got this wrong because what the Bible says doesn't fit what we know actually happened."

That kind of double-standard is simply unfair and bad scholarship. The Bible needs to be considered on a level playing field.

Deal With The Real

One of the ways we defend the reliability of the Bible is by confirming that the skeptics are dealing with what the Bible actually says and not a misunderstanding of it or an outright fabrication that they mistakenly believe is in there.

As a parent of two daughters, I can tell you from personal experience how important this is. Normally, my girls get along great, but as with any kids, there are the occasional disagreements. I usually try to let them work these disagreements out themselves because I know how important it is for them to learn how to do this, but sometimes I feel that I need to get involved, usually when I sense that there's some kind of miscommunication going on. When I do get involved, one of the first things I have to figure out is *who said what exactly*? The second thing I have to figure out is *what exactly was meant by that*?

So I might ask Lynae, "Why are you so upset?" And her answer might be "Because she said she doesn't like to play with me!"

"Rochelle," I ask my eldest, "did you say that you don't like playing with her?"

"No," Rochelle replies, "I said that when she starts making up new rules and then using them without telling me what they are, I don't like playing with her."

See, now I understand what was actually said and what Rochelle meant by it, and I can proceed accordingly. But if I had disciplined Rochelle for "being mean to your little sister" simply based on Lynae's recollection of the argument, that wouldn't have been fair. I needed to make sure I was evaluating Rochelle's actual statement rather than just someone else's faulty memory of it.

Many objections to the reliability of the Bible are based on misunderstandings of what the Bible actually says or what it means by what it says.

Sometimes people attack the Bible based on pure fabrication. For instance, I've heard people say that the Bible contains a contradiction because it says Jesus was born on December 25, but that he was actually born during the spring.[73] But of course the Bible doesn't say Jesus was born on December 25 – that's just the date that we have chosen to celebrate his birth!

Other objections are based on misinterpretations of the Bible. For instance, a common objection to the Bible is that it "encourages slavery." Is this true? Actually, no, it's not true at all. What the Bible does is *regulate the treatment* of slaves so that they would not be abused. This isn't the same thing as prohibiting slavery, of course, but it's a long way from *encouraging* slavery. Moreover, it could be argued that the Bible actually discourages slavery because the regulations it places on slave owners made owning slaves a burden.

But why not just come out and say "don't own slaves" if that is what the Bible intended? Well, that's a complicated question. To understand the answer, we would have to understand a great deal about what slavery was and was not in the ancient world. We tend to hear the word "slave" and think of pre-Civil War America, but that's really not what "slave" meant in the ancient Jewish or Christian world. In fact, many scholars today object to using the word "slave" as a translation for the underlying Hebrew and Greek words and argue instead that "servant" is a much more appropriate translation. In fact, it

---

[73] The spring being the most likely time that shepherds would have been spending the nights out in the fields with their flocks.

seems to me that "slavery" in the Biblical sense was quite similar to something we call "patronage," whereby individuals served a family in various ways in return for food and shelter. After all, according to the Bible, "slaves" had to be well-fed, given days off, could not be physically mistreated and had legal rights quite similar to those of "slave"-owners.

My point is simply that when someone objects to the Bible because it "encourages slavery," they simply don't know what the Bible actually says on that subject. That is, they are objecting to either a mis-quote or a mis-interpretation of the Bible.

In the same way that we can't attack someone for saying something without knowing if they actually said it, we can't object to things the Bible says until we are sure the Bible actually said them and meant them the way we've taken them.

Starting From The Proper Perspective – Making Points In The Bible's Favor

When it comes to the reliability of the Bible, there are a number of things that can be said that might cause skeptics to rethink their position.

It's important to remember that no-one can ever prove that the Bible is reliable, let alone inerrant. If someone is dead-set on distrusting the Bible, there's really nothing you can do to change their mind. This is mostly due to the fact that there is no corroborating evidence for much of what the Bible claims. This is to be expected. The Bible was written a long time ago and during a period of history without cameras or video recorders. What we know of events from that period is almost entirely based on what ancient writers wrote about those events. This is true not only of the Bible but of every other historical text.

Think about this: imagine your friend says to you "I saw a coyote in the field behind my house today." Now, your friend didn't get a picture of the coyote or catch a few seconds of video on his cell phone, so there's no evidence that he's telling the truth. The question is, would you believe him or not?

Chances are your answer is "it depends." What would it depend on? Well, it might depend on several things: whether or not you've seen coyotes there yourself, whether or not you've heard other people say they've seen coyotes there and, most importantly, whether or not you trust your friend. If you don't trust him, there's nothing he can do to convince you that he actually saw a coyote. On the other hand, if you do generally trust him, you're probably going to assume that he's telling the truth unless evidence to the contrary surfaces.

If you don't trust your friend, that's pretty much the end of it. You won't explore whether or not there's any reason to believe him. On the other hand, if you're at least open to the possibility that he's telling you the truth, you might go looking to see if there's anything to back up his story.

Imagine that you go out in the field with your friend and you find some fresh paw-prints that look like coyote tracks and some fur on a thorn bush that looks like coyote hair. Have you proven that your friend saw a coyote? No, but you've found evidence that is consistent with your friend's story, making you far more likely to believe that he actually saw what he said he saw.

In the same way, if someone is dead-set against trusting the Bible, you really can't prove to them that the Bible is reliable. They won't even listen. However, if you're dealing with someone who is genuinely interested in whether or not the Bible is reliable, there are a number of things that demonstrate that the Bible has a track record that gives us good reason to trust it. This doesn't mean that we can prove everything in the Bible actually happened, but when someone or something has a history of demonstrated reliability, you tend to pay attention to what they say, even when you have no immediate way of substantiating their claims.

Archaeology

Archaeology cannot prove any historical claim to be true. The most archaeology can do is confirm some details of historical accounts or, in some cases, disprove an ancient account. If an ancient Egyptian historian wrote that Pharaoh Tutencampote was 9 feet tall, and archaeologists excavated the pharaoh's tomb and found his 4'7" mummy, we would know that the Egyptian historian had gotten his facts wrong – or that he had made his "facts" up.

Archaeology can never prove that Jesus rose from the dead. If we found his tomb and his body inside the tomb, this would prove that the Gospels' claims of Jesus' resurrection are false,[74] of course, but the lack of such a tomb doesn't really count as good evidence that the resurrection happened.

---

[74] This is exactly what a recent special on the Discovery Channel claimed to have discovered. However, on closer inspection, even strongly anti-Christian scholars determined that this claim was unfounded. See "The Lost Tomb of Jesus?" at www.shepherdproject.com/resources

However, there are other archaeological considerations here. When Jesus' disciples began claiming that Jesus had risen from the dead, his enemies had both the means and the motive to prove them wrong: all they had to do was open up the tomb and show people that the body was still there. It seems likely to me that they would have then made this tomb a sort of prominent tourist attraction as a way of stamping out the fledgling Christian movement. The fact that we have no evidence of such a thing suggests – though it certainly doesn't prove – that the Jewish authorities weren't able to produce a body or an occupied tomb.

On the other hand, recent archaeological discoveries in Jerusalem include an ossuary (bone box) with the words "James, son of Joseph, brother of Jesus." While this discovery has been hotly contested among archaeologists, there is good reason to think that this is an authentic 1st-century ossuary. Why is this significant? Because if authentic, it confirms some of the claims from the Bible: James, the brother (or half-brother, to be technical) of Jesus was a real person and both of them had a father named Joseph. More importantly, the fact that Jesus' name is listed on the ossuary is evidence that this Jesus was a very important person. Otherwise, why list him on the box? The only time a brother was listed in such a manner was when the brother was famous.

In a similar way, archaeology cannot prove that David defeated Goliath with a sling. However, archaeology has confirmed that David was a real king of Israel and that he ruled during the same time period that the Bible claims he did.

Archaeology cannot prove that Moses parted the Red Sea, but it has unearthed evidence that there were Israelite slaves in

Egypt during the period the Bible claims they were there.[75] Archaeology cannot prove that God brought down the walls of Jericho with trumpets, but it has demonstrated that the walls of the city were destroyed in a way that is perfectly consistent with the biblical description.[76] The simple truth is that no archaeological evidence has ever come to light which disproves any claim of the Bible. On the contrary, archaeological discoveries have time and again confirmed myriad details of biblical accounts, leading those who are genuinely curious to believe that the Bible can be trusted in regards to other issues which cannot be so easily substantiated.

The Proof Is <u>Not</u> In The Pudding

Okay, I'm not even sure what that phrase means, but it seemed like a great way to introduce this topic! Whereas archaeology depends on the presence of certain things to demon-

---

[75] M. Bietak, *Avaris and Piramesse: Archaeological Exploration in the Eastern Nile Delta*, (London: The British Academy, 1986); "Der Friedhof in einem Palastgarten aus der Zeit des spten Mittleren Riches und andere Forschungsergebnisse aus dem stlichen Nildelta (Tell el-Daba 1984-1987)," *Agypten und Levante* 2 (1991a), 47-75; "Egypt and Canaan During the Middle Bronze Age," *Bulletin of the American Schools of Oriental Research*, 281 (1991b), 27-72; *Avaris: The Capital of the Hyksos*, (London: British Museum Press, 1996).

[76] Bryant G. Wood, "Did the Israelites Conquer Jericho? A New Look at the Archaeological Evidence", *Biblical Archaeology Review*, March/April 1990, 44-58.

strate the reliability of the Bible, the absence of other things in the Bible has the same impact.

Here's what I mean: if the Bible were made up, there are certain things that we would expect to find but don't. For instance, if the Gospels had been made up, then why didn't the authors invent Jesus' sayings that answered important questions the early Church faced? The book of Acts makes it clear that the leadership of the early Church had a huge debate over whether or not to circumcise[77] the Gentile (non-Jewish) converts to Christianity (Acts 15). Keep in mind that all of the earliest followers of Jesus were Jews and they didn't think that had changed. After all, they merely believed that the Jewish man, Jesus, was the long-awaited Jewish Messiah. They didn't think they were seeing the start of a new religion – they thought they were seeing the fulfillment of an old one. So when Gentiles started believing in Jesus, the early Church leadership tended to think that they should become Jews, which required circumcision. Not surprisingly, the Gentile believers weren't tremendously excited about this, and a huge debate broke out. To circumcise or not to circumcise, that was the question. The reason it was such a difficult question, though, was because Jesus hadn't given any instruction about it. Think about it: if Jesus had simply said "Thou shalt not circumciseth the Gentiles," that would have been the end of the debate. But we have no record of Jesus ever addressing the subject of circumcision at all.

---

[77] OK, not a pleasant subject, but just in case you're not familiar with the term: circumcision is the act by which the foreskin of a male penis is surgically removed.

Do you see what I'm getting at? If the Gospels contained fabrications, if they had invented the teachings of Jesus as some skeptics claim, then why in the world didn't they invent teachings of Jesus that would have settled this debate that was dividing the early Church? You can't say that the Gospels were written before this debate became an issue in the Church because they weren't. This debate was happening in the church in the 40s or 50s A.D., but the first Gospel wasn't written until the early 60s.

Similarly, there are lots of other issues that God's people have struggled with precisely because there are no biblical passages which settle the debate. What exactly does it mean to keep the Sabbath holy (a major debate for Jews in Jesus' day)? How can God be both one God yet three persons? How could Jesus be both human and divine? These are the sorts of things that could easily have been settled if someone felt free to make up a revelation or a teaching from Jesus. The fact that we have no definitive statements on such issues indicates that the writers of the Bible didn't feel free to make them up.

If someone refuses to make up answers to important questions, then this suggests that the answers they do give are reliable.

Awkward Stuff

Along these same lines, the fact that the Bible contains some awkward stuff suggests that the authors of the Bible were sticklers for truth and only the truth.

For instance, the Gospels of Matthew and Luke both contain genealogies of Jesus – but they're different. How can that be? Well, some skeptics have argued that these two different genealogies for the same person are simply proof that the Bible is unreliable. But if one of the Gospel writers got the genealogy wrong, why didn't someone fix it? Why did they let two different genealogies continue to exist side by side in the canon of Scripture? It seems that if the Church felt free to fabricate or otherwise alter the Biblical text they would have taken care of this awkward situation. Yet they didn't. Why?

It seems to me that there are three possibilities:

1. They were too stupid to realize the contradiction.

2. They recognized the contradiction but were afraid to mess with the Bible.

3. They didn't see the two genealogies as a contradiction because they knew something we don't know.

Option #1 just won't work. Option #2 is interesting in that, even if true, it implies that no one was willing to change the biblical text. So, contrary to what many skeptics suggest, there's simply no good evidence that the Bible has been altered over the years. But what about option #3? Is that possible? It is. In fact, it is likely that the earliest readers of the Gospels would have understood that Luke and Matthew were both being selective in the names they gave in order to highlight a particular feature of Jesus' nature.[78]

---

[78] Remember the purpose of Matthew's genealogy that we discussed earlier?

Is this a completely satisfying answer to the question of why the two genealogies differ somewhat? It depends on whether or not you've already decided that the Bible is unreliable. If you think it's unreliable and don't want to hear anything to the contrary, you'll reject this explanation without any thought whatsoever. On the other hand, if you're at least open to the possibility that the Bible is reliable, you'll have to give it some serious thought. And one of the things that serious thought will reveal is the realization that the early Church could have easily "fixed" this awkwardness, and the fact that they didn't suggests that they didn't think it needed fixing.

So, oddly enough, many of the awkward things in the Bible that skeptics use as an excuse for distrusting it are actually reasons to trust it! In the end it often comes down to saying "I can either assume that I'm right and the Bible is untrustworthy, or that the Bible is trustworthy and I simply don't understand it completely."

Speaking of awkward stuff, the Bible also contains a number of things that are downright embarrassing. For instance, when you read in the Bible about Peter, the first and possibly greatest leader of the Christian church, he's kind of...well, he's kind of a dork. I mean, he does some really great stuff, but he also messes up a lot. Sure he's the guy who recognized who Jesus was:

> Simon Peter answered, "You are the Christ, the Son of the living God." Jesus replied, "Blessed are you, Simon son of Jonah, for this was not revealed to you by man, but by my Father in heaven.
>
> (Matthew 16:16-17)

But in the very next passage, when Jesus began to talk about dying for the sins of the world, Peter told him to stop talking like that and Jesus said:

> *"Get behind me, Satan! You are a stumbling block to me; you do not have in mind the things of God, but the things of men."*
> (Matthew 16:23)

So here the leader of the early church goes from being the first disciple to really "get" Jesus because God talks to him to being the devil! Listen, if you're making stuff up, do you think that you would make up Jesus calling your most important church leader Satan? I don't think so.

And actually, you know what? It's not entirely clear that Peter was the first one to really understand who Jesus was. The Gospel of John tells us that a woman named Martha came to the same conclusion, and it's not entirely clear whose realization came first:

> *"Yes, Lord," she told him, "I believe that you are the Christ, the Son of God, who was to come into the world."*
> (John 11:27)

So here we have a woman, who "got" Jesus perhaps before any of his closest disciples did. That's a bit embarrassing in a society where women were given very little respect. But it gets "worse" from a societal perspective: the Bible also says that women were the first people to meet Jesus after he rose from the dead! Not men, women! This is just not the sort of thing you make up if you're fabricating stories to give your organization credibility.

Or what about David? You remember David, right? The giant-killer? The author of most of the Psalms? The "man after God's own heart"? Well, read in 2 Samuel 11-12 about how he shirked his duties, raped a woman and got her pregnant, tried to cover it up and, when that failed, had her husband murdered. Awkward! Why would you make that kind of thing up about your religious heroes? You wouldn't. You would only report that kind of thing if it was true. By the way, how could David be called a man after God's own heart if he did something like this? Because he repented. Confronted with his sin, he confessed it, turned from it and threw himself on the mercy of God for forgiveness, which God granted. David wasn't a man after God's own heart because he was perfect; he was a man after God's own heart because he recognized his imperfection and sin, and because he continually turned away from his sin and back to God.

If the Bible can be so brutally honest even about the failures of its greatest heroes, it can be trusted to tell us the truth about everything.

When a friend, who has never lied to you, even when the truth is embarrassing, tells you something, even something pretty incredible, you believe them. When someone has proven their reliability over and over again, you assume their trustworthiness, at least as a starting point for future interactions. In the same way, when all the facts are laid on the table and rationally considered, there is a great deal to be said in favor of the reliability of the Bible. Does this mean that we have proven the reliability of the Bible in everything? No, of course not, but it does suggest that rather than assuming the Bible to be unreliable, it is more rational to assume that the Bible is reliable. That's where the evidence points.

Dealing With Specific Issues

Here's how most of my conversations about the reliability of the Bible with skeptics go:

> Skeptic: "So you really think the Bible is accurate and reliable?"
>
> Me: "Yes, I do."
>
> Skeptic: "But how can you believe that with all the contradictions and errors in the Bible?"
>
> Me: "Like what?"
>
> Skeptic: "What do you mean?"
>
> Me: "I mean, what contradictions and errors are you thinking of?"
>
> Skeptic: "You know, all the places where one part of the Bible says the opposite of what another part says."
>
> Me: "Yeah, I know what a contradiction is. I'm just wondering what, specifically, you might be thinking of."
>
> Skeptic: "Well, how about... um... maybe where... uh... you know, the place where it... um..."

166 | Defending The Bible

For most people, their refusal to believe that the Bible is accurate and reliable is a smokescreen. They simply don't want to believe the Bible and so they've justified their unbelief with another, equally-unfounded belief: that the Bible is full of errors and contradictions. But ask them for specific examples and most people can't come up with even one.

More often than not, if they do try something specific, they'll say something like, "Well what about where the Israelites ate food that fell out of the sky while they were in the desert? That's ridiculous!" But see, what they're talking about here isn't a contradiction or even a supposed error; it's just something they find hard to believe. True, the Bible contains a great deal that is hard to believe if you're looking at it from an anti-supernatural perspective. Anti-supernaturalism is the belief that supernatural things don't happen. If you read the Bible through this lens, then the Bible will be hard to trust. After all, it speaks about any number of things that can only be explained by supernatural causes. If you don't believe in anything supernatural, then you have to deny anything that can only have a supernatural cause. But this doesn't mean the Bible is contradictory or wrong. It just means that you can't believe the Bible and also believe in anti-supernaturalism. If anti-supernaturalism is right, then the Bible can't be right. But since there's absolutely no proof that anti-supernaturalism is right and there is lots of evidence that the Bible is reliable, which one makes more sense to believe?

Now this is not to say that no-one will ever have a legitimate question or objection to the reliability of the Bible. By "legitimate" I primarily mean objections that remain after we've made sure the playing field is level and we're dealing with something the Bible actually says vs. something someone only thinks the Bible says.

When we encounter legitimate objections to the reliability of the Bible, here's what we do:

1. *Acknowledge the validity of the question.*

Just blowing off a hard question about the Bible isn't helpful. This just communicates to people that we're not willing to take them or their questions seriously. Instead, admit that the question is valid and, if the question is difficult to answer, say that. This will go a long way in establishing a healthy foundation for the conversation.

2. *If you know the answer to the question, explain the answer clearly and respectfully.*

One of the things you'll find as you defend the Bible is that most skeptics have the same basic questions. Once you've developed the ability to answer those questions you'll be able to use the answers over and over again.

3. *If you don't know the answer to the question, admit it.*

Don't try to fake your way through it. If you don't know the answer, just say so. You can always explain that you have some good reasons for approaching the Bible from a starting point of trust (see above) and that this is why a question you don't have the answer to doesn't bother you too much. Then, if you have some thoughts on the answer to their question, share them, but do so from a position of humility: *"you know, I don't really know what the answer to that question is. I have a couple of ideas, though. Can I share them with you?"*

Interestingly, my experience has been that this approach sometimes has more positive impact than actually having great answers. Sometimes having pre-packaged answers, especially if we're arrogant in the way we share them, makes people think that we're just hiding behind memorized lessons because we're afraid of actually facing the difficult questions about the Bible. Conversely, sharing our ignorance about a particular question and letting them see our thought process as we work through a possible answer communicates that our belief is not rigid and unthinking but is instead fluid and well-grounded.

4. If you don't know the answer, do some research and get back to the question-asker.

While this book contains a number of answers to common questions about the Bible, we obviously haven't covered everything you might be asked. But there are lots of good resources out there to help you address specific questions. A good place to start looking for reliable resources on just about any question you might be asked about the Bible is:

shepherdproject.com/resources

This website contains an ever-growing database of resources to help you with specific questions you might be asked. And if you can't find an answer there to the question you're researching, you can post the question and we'll get to work on it for you!

Once you understand the answer to the question, share it with the person who asked. The fact that you took their question seriously enough to research an answer will communicate a great deal to them.

Wrapping It All Up

Obviously, I haven't attempted to answer each and every potential objection that skeptics have raised against the Bible. There simply isn't room here to do that. Instead, what I've tried to do is provide a way of thinking about defending the Bible that will serve as a foundation on which you can build a defense of particular issues.

So when someone asks, "But what about _____?" you'll be able to start by making sure the challenge is based on reasonable standards, standards that can be – and are – applied to other historical documents (*leveling the playing field*). You'll be able to look critically at the objection and make sure that it deals with what the Bible actually says, rather than with a myth, a mis-reading or a mis-interpretation of it (*deal with the real*). You'll be able to communicate the reasons why we should start from a position of trust rather than mis-trust of the Bible (*starting from the proper perspective*). And finally, you'll know how to go about answering questions that remain after the first three steps have been followed.

Then & Now

When I walked into that college English class, I had no real idea what I was in for. I knew I believed the Bible, but I didn't really know why. Actually, it might be more accurate to say that I *thought* I believed the Bible. I didn't really understand what the Bible was, how we got it or why it could be trusted enough to say that I really "believed" the Bible.

Since then, I've gone through periods of questioning, studying, pondering and even challenging. I've studied in some environments that were committed to the inerrancy and authority of the Bible and in environments that were not committed to these things.

In the end, however, what began in that college class was a journey that I could never have imagined, but one that I'm so glad I've been on. Over the years as my understanding of God's Word has deepened, so has my trust in it and in Him.

I am convinced that you will have this same experience if you will only let God's Word do what it promises to do:

> *All Scripture is God-breathed and is useful for teaching, rebuking, correcting and training in righteousness, so that the man of God may be thoroughly equipped for every good work.*
>
> (2 Timothy 3:16-17)

For further resources in answering specific questions about the Bible or the Christian faith in general, visit the ever-growing database of resources at:

www.shepherdproject.com

Index Of Scriptures Cited

Ephesians 5:6, 24
Ephesians 6:10-12, 136
1 Thessalonians 2:16, 25
2 Timothy 3:16-17, 43, 68,
183
Hebrews 4:12, 34
James, 91

Revelation 2:1-4, 41
Revelation 3:14-16, 142
Revelation 3:19, 138
Revelation 11:3-10, 129
Revelation 11:10, 128
Revelation 15:7, 25

Index Of Works Cited

Anderson, Robert, *The Coming Prince* (New York: Cosimo Classics, 2007 reprint).

Aune, D.E., "On the Origins of the 'Council of Javneh' Myth", *Journal of Biblical Literature*, 110:3 (1991).

Bauckham, Richard, *Jesus and the Eyewitnesses: The Gospels as Eyewitness Testimony* (Grand Rapids: William B. Eerdmans Publishing Company, 2006).

Beckwith, Roger, *T he Old Testament Canon of the New Testament Church* (Grand Rapids: William B. Eerdmans Publishing Company, 1985).

Bietak, M., *Avaris and Piramesse: Archaeological Exploration in the Eastern Nile Delta*, (London: The British Academy, 1986); "Der Friedhof in einem Palastgarten aus der Zeit des spten Mittleren Riches und andere Forschungsergebnisse aus dem stlichen Nildelta (Tell el-Daba 1984-1987)," *Agypten und Levante* 2 (1991a), 47-75; "Egypt and Canaan During the Middle Bronze Age," *Bulletin of the American Schools of Oriental Research*, 281 (1991b), 27-72; *Avaris: The Capital of the Hyksos*, (London: British Museum Press, 1996).

Biran, Avraham and Joseph Naveh, "An Aramaic Stele Fragment from Tel Dan," *Israel Exploration Journal* 43 (1993), 81-98. Dawkins, Richard, *The God Delusion* (London: Bantam Books, 2006).

Bock, Darrell L., *The Missing Gospels: Unearthing the Truth Behind Alternative Christianities* (Nashville: Thomas Nelson Books, Inc., 2006).

Eilat, Mazar, "Did I Find King David's Palace?", *Biblical Archaeology Review* 32:1 (2006), 16-27, 70.

Gerberding, R. and J. H. Moran Cruz, *Medieval Worlds* (New York: Houghton Mifflin Company, 2004).

Graetz, Heinrich H., *Kohelet oder der Salomonische Prediger* (Leipzig: Winter, 1871).

Grant, Robert M. *The Formation of the New Testament.* (New York: Harper & Row, 1965).

Hitchens, Christopher, *God Is Not Great: How Religion Poisons Everything* (New York: Twelve Books, 2007)

Johnson, Alan, "Revelation" in *EBC* 12 (Grand Rapids: Zondervan Publishing House, 1981).

Schaff, Philip and Henry Wace, *Nicene and Post-Nicene Fathers,* IV (2nd series), (Grand Rapids, MI: Eerdmans, 1978).

Trobisch, David, *The First Edition of the New Testament* (New York: Oxford University Press, 2000).

Thiele, Edwin, *The Mysterious Numbers of the Hebrew Kings* (Grand Rapids: Zondervan, 1983).

Walls, Andrew F., "The Canon of the New Testament" in *The Expositor's Bible Commentary* (Grand Rapids: Zondervan Publishing Company, 1984), 1:638.

Wood, Bryant G., "Did the Israelites Conquer Jericho? A New Look at the Archaeological Evidence", *Biblical Archaeology Review*, March/April (1990), 44-58.

About The Author

Craig Smith is a popular speaker and teacher, in-demand around the world for his ability to engage audiences and take them deep into Truth. He holds a Ph.D. in Biblical Studies from Bristol University, UK.

Craig is an adjunct professor of Biblical Studies and Christian Doctrine at Denver Theological Seminary and is the executive director of the Shepherd Project, a parachurch ministry focused on helping Christians maximize their impact on culture for the sake of Christ and his Kingdom.

Craig speaks to thousands of people every year at a wide variety of events, from youth retreats to theological conferences. For booking information, contact Shepherd Project Ministries at www.shepherdproject.com.

LaVergne, TN USA
22 July 2010
190523LV00004B/30/P